D0998213

Formerly

The^Stressed Vegan

Ultimate Guide To Optimal Health
Beat Stress-Related Diseases Naturally

11/16/18   **Taly Cotler**

Dear Julie

To your health!

Love

Taly Cotl

Copyright © Taly Cotler, 2018.

All rights reserved.

Without limiting the right under copyright reserved above, no part of this publication may be reproduced, stored in or introduced into a retrieval system, or transmitted, in any form, or by any means(electronic, mechanical, photocopying, recording, or otherwise), without the prior written permission of the copyright owner and the above publisher of this book.

The scanning, uploading, and distribution of this book via the internet or via any other means without the permission of the author is illegal and punishable by law. Please purchase only authorized electronic additions, and do not participate in or encourage electronic piracy of copyrighted materials. Your support of the author's rights is appreciated.

ISBN: 978-1-7327458-0-3 (Printed Version)
ISBN: 978-1-7327458-1-0 (E-Book)

Reviewed and edited by Thressa D. Smith, PhD.
Book cover and design done by Amit Dey.
Published by Taly Cotler.

The Formerly Stressed Vegan
Ultimate Guide To Optimal Health
Beat Stress-Related Diseases Naturally/Taly Cotler.

Contents

Disclaimer

This book details the author's personal experiences with and opinions about health and wellness. The author is not a healthcare provider. The author and publisher are providing this book and its contents on an "as is" basis and make no representations or warranties of any kind with respect to this book or its contents.

The author and publisher disclaim all such representations and warranties, including healthcare for a particular purpose. In addition, the author and publisher do not represent or warrant that the information accessible via this book is accurate, complete or current. The statements made about products and services have not been evaluated by the U.S. Food and Drug Administration. They are not intended to diagnose, treat, cure, or prevent any condition or disease. Please consult with your own physician or healthcare specialist regarding the suggestions and recommendations made in this book. Neither the author nor the publisher, or any authors, contributors, or other representatives will be liable for any damages arising out of or in connection with the use of this book.

You understand that this book is not intended as a substitute for consultation with a licensed healthcare practitioner, such as your physician. Before you begin any healthcare program, or change your lifestyle in any way, consult your physician or another licensed healthcare practitioner to ensure that you are in good health and that the examples contained in this book will not harm you. This book provides content related to physical and/or mental health issues. As such, use of this book implies your acceptance of this disclaimer.

Dedication

I thank my family and especially my intuitive and courageous daughter, Michelle Cotler, for helping me and supporting me through this ordeal and contributing to my recovery. Throughout my journey to optimal health, Michelle was extremely supportive and encouraging; she was always by my side, trying to help me to feel better. I dedicate this book to her, Michelle, the smartest, most intuitive, and mature young woman I have ever known. I am so grateful for her and so proud to be her Mom.

Preface

Throughout my school years, I consistently excelled in mathematics, science, and computer sciences. Geometry and algebra? They were easy for me. I could solve arithmetic calculations in my mind, without pencil and paper. By contrast, my least favorite subject was language arts. Sure, I could write an essay, but it never came out right, and it always took a long time to complete. Writing has always been my least favorite thing to do. So the thought of writing a short story, let alone an entire book, had never crossed my mind.

However, in more recent years, I was forced to develop writing skills for a project I was working on. I practiced writing so much that it finally became almost second nature. Still, the fact that I wrote my first book is beyond my belief. I can say that I have reached a sense of self-fulfillment at this stage of my life. My dominant, rational, left brain is finally attaining a balance with my newly explored, creative, right brain.

Beginning at a very early age, I read health-related books and researched various health-related topics. About ten years ago, prior to my health challenge, I felt that I had gained sufficient knowledge on these subjects to write a book. However, the task of sitting down and writing was always delayed by family obligations, my career, and, of course, my dislike for writing.

Both my kids are now grown and no longer live with me, so I have some free time. I was never a storyteller, but out of the blue a couple of years ago, thoughts and words about my health challenge as well as the research that I have done over the years regarding health and wellness just started coming to me. What I have learned during my challenging health ordeal is not something to be kept hidden behind closed doors. I deeply and profoundly feel that all the health and wellness-related knowledge, personal experience, and life-long research that I have accumulated is something that must be shared with others.

Skeptics may say, "Oh, but how can you write a book about health? You're not a doctor." I agree; I am by no means a doctor, nor do I ever pretend to be. I am, instead, presenting health advice from a very different perspective, that of someone with extensive personal experience with a substantial health challenge who recovered long-term optimal health naturally, without the use of conventional medicine.

"Anyone who doesn't believe in miracles
is not a realist."

— David Ben Gurion

Taly Cotler,
The Stressed Vegan

CHAPTER 1

My Story

Let's start with a brief background and description of the journey that led to my writing this book. I currently reside in south Florida, although I was born and raised in Israel. At a young age, I read many health-related books and learned about the correlation between food and health. The healthier and less processed foods we eat, the healthier we are. For example, red meat can be harmful to our bodies, but fruits and vegetables are beneficial. I never liked the taste or consistency of red meat or chicken. Therefore, I eliminated both from my diet at the age of twelve and became a vegetarian. Growing up in Israel, where the Mediterranean diet is widely prevalent, I found it fairly easy to follow a vegetarian diet.

My entire life I have been active, eaten a healthy diet, exercised, and stayed fit. I was full of energy, motivated, ambitious, and on the go. I raised two kids, mostly by myself, and made sure that they came first, that is, my first priority was ensuring all their needs were met. So I experienced stress not only from being a single parent but also from managing a full-time job and other commitments.

My career was in information technology, specifically in software engineering, which requires a high level of focus, accuracy, attention to detail, and problem-solving skills. This career alone can be very stressful. But in addition to my career and my type A personality, I had family obligations to fulfill, and I had gone back to school. My responsibilities were overwhelming. I was overworked and busy nonstop. I found little time to relax or take a vacation. There is no doubt that I spread myself too thin, and at some point, it all became too much. In my late 30s, I developed a syndrome called adrenal fatigue. In this syndrome, the level of cortisol, which is a stress hormone, is often too low, and the adrenal gland function is below the necessary level. Adrenal fatigue is accompanied by symptoms of extreme fatigue and exhaustion that do not improve with sleep. Because of this debilitating condition, I could no longer be under any stress nor could I keep up with the demands of my family and career. It was extremely frustrating and challenging to have so much to do and yet no energy to do it. It was like I was trying to drive a car in the fast lane without any gasoline. An integrative health care provider helped me to deal with the condition. Although I noticed some improvement, I was not at a point that I would have liked to be, and I certainly was not functioning at an optimal level.

The constant stress I had experienced over a prolonged time eventually took a toll on my body. One night in my early 40s, shortly after I fell asleep, I suddenly woke up with severe pressure in my chest. My heart rate was so high that I thought I was having a heart attack. My blood pressure was elevated, I was in constant pain, and I felt dizzy and lightheaded. I was taken to the emergency department at a local hospital, where they ran various diagnostic tests that all came back normal. I was told, "You probably had a panic attack," and was sent home.

I thought, *this cannot be the case because I have never experienced a panic attack and there is no reason that I should have one.* Two days later, the same thing happened: chest pressure and pain, elevated heart rate and blood pressure, and dizziness. Once again, I was taken to the emergency department, had more tests, and was sent home. For the next few months, I experienced those episodes regularly. The next time I called 911 to request an ambulance, two police officers showed up at my home along with the paramedics. They were all totally convinced that I was having panic attacks but was so mentally unstable that I was repeatedly and unnecessarily calling for an ambulance. I was furious that they didn't take me seriously. It took some time to convince them that I was in excruciating pain. However, once the police officers saw my elevated heart rate, they instructed the paramedics to take me to the emergency department. This time, I asked to go to a different hospital, hoping to get better care because I was desperate to feel better.

I was hospitalized for fourteen days. The doctors ran a battery of diagnostic tests, all of which came back with normal results. Finally, a non-traditional table tilt test determined that I had postural orthostatic tachycardia syndrome or POTS. This is a condition in which the heart rate is elevated significantly on standing, sometimes up to 150 beats per minute without any exertion. I was never told what had suddenly caused the syndrome to appear. In addition, I had experienced symptoms that did not fall under the POTS description. I was not thrilled with their lack of answers nor with the treatment protocol that was suggested to me.

Because my heart rate was so elevated, I was prescribed blood pressure medication to keep it under control. However, because I have normal blood pressure (100/65), the medication to lower my blood pressure led to adverse effects. I was prescribed many different medications for the various symptoms that I had experienced. However, this host of medication not only did not help, it exacerbated the situation. I was extremely frustrated by a lack of sleep, the lack of an accurate diagnosis, a misdiagnosis, and the lack of proper treatment by conventional medicine doctors.

I continued to experience elevated heart rate, increased blood pressure, severe pressure in my chest, constant dizziness, lightheadedness, and persistent hunger. The dizziness was severe; I could not stand up because my heart rate would increase to 150 beats per minute the second I stood. As a result, I was bed ridden for a very long time and I used a wheelchair to move around. I went to conventional medical specialists, but not one of them was able to properly diagnose my condition. I was misdiagnosed with agoraphobia, panic attacks, depression, anxiety, and more. I absolutely disagreed with each of these misdiagnoses. For example, I had always been a happy and outgoing person who liked to travel the world, so by no means did I have agoraphobia. The doctors prescribed additional medications (I was up to seven by then) that were not helpful at all and further exacerbated my symptoms. I was taking more medications during that ordeal than I had taken throughout my entire life.

It was so frustrating to know that something was wrong with my body, but the medical doctors could not give me an accurate diagnosis. I was particularly upset that I had led such a healthy lifestyle and was so energetic before my whole world fell apart in an instant. There was no comparison between this ordeal and the adrenal fatigue I had experienced in my 30s. This ordeal was much more severe and serious.

Between having those episodes of high blood pressure and elevated heart rate, it felt as though something that was out of my control had taken over my body. I had chronic insomnia and great difficulty falling asleep. The loud and fast sound of my heartbeat in my ears also kept me from getting much sleep. For almost a year, I was lucky to get one or two hours of sleep per night. I felt tired and wired at the same time, and I just could not get my heart rate to come down. Although I was absolutely exhausted, my body would not slow down and go to sleep. I felt like the energizer bunny battery, going and going nonstop.

I had never felt that bad or experienced anything like that before. I wanted to know what was happening with my health and to receive an accurate diagnosis and treatment plan so that I could feel better. I constantly feared that my condition could not be reversed. I was especially concerned about my daughter, Michelle, who was only 11 years old at the time. I knew that she was worried about me and that I had to be strong for her. I became more determined than ever to overcome this health challenge. My daughter was young, and she needed me healthy.

I expressed my concern to the doctors that the medications were not helping and that I was actually feeling worse. I asked them,

"What about holistic doctor practitioners who can look further into the cause of this health crisis?" But the doctors referred to holistic practitioners as quacks, not "real" doctors. I got a clear message to stay away from holistic medicine practitioners, to the point that I became skeptical of them myself. Doctors spend many years studying and practicing medicine, right? So who am I to think I can compete with their knowledge and ability?

However, I was puzzled as to how conventional medicine doctors could criticize and doubt holistic doctors if they themselves could not fully diagnose or treat me. I was torn between conventional medicine and holistic medicine, not sure who to seek for help. Although the doctors insisted that I would have to take these medications for the rest of my life as well as use a wheelchair, I thought, *No way*! Using a wheelchair at 40 years of age and taking medications for the rest of my life was not what I considered a solution.

One day I decided to take things into my own hands and research this further. I asked my daughter to get me several of my natural health-related books from the other room. I read through some of them. I came to the conclusion that the body can reverse illness and heal itself if given the right nutrients. I also concluded that disease is caused by a toxic overload; so it is crucial to detox the body on a regular basis. Although I had come to these important conclusions, I was fearful of taking any chances with my health on my own, and I did not know how to go about letting my body heal itself. As I was pondering all this, I asked my daughter to place the books on my dresser. She did and then left the room. I noticed that she had stacked all of the books with their titles facing the wall except one book. Its title faced me. It was called *Healing without Medications*. I kept staring at it, wondering why that specific book was placed like that. In the ensuing days, the universe showed me more signs, until finally no doubt was left in my mind. I was determined to try a holistic approach to address my debilitating condition. I could not know at the time that this ended up being one of the best decisions of my life.

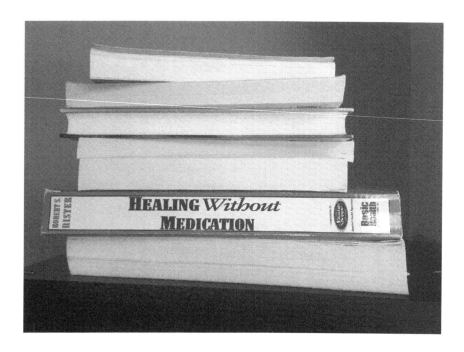

I am so thankful for my intuitive and amazing daughter who helped me to find the road to recovery. Honestly, I am not surprised by what Michelle did because she had great intuition at a very young age. For instance, I took her to a book store when she was only 18 months old. She pulled a book out of a pile of about fifty different books and insisted that I buy it. It was called *The Seat of the Soul* by Gary Zukav. To this day, I still have that book. Miracles DO happen! I believe this. So when Michelle placed that book title facing me, right then and there, I had no more doubts. I decided to give the holistic way of healing a chance. Although I did not know it at the time, it was very fortunate that I did not continue the medical protocol suggested by the conventional medicine doctors.

My condition was soon accurately diagnosed by a holistic medicine practitioner in Arizona. Dr. W. said that I had a very advanced stage of adrenal fatigue. The cortisol level in my body was much higher than the normal range, indicating that I was totally burned out. The adrenal fatigue had led to the POTS symptoms. The additional symptoms that I had experienced were related to something called a thyroid storm. Dr. W. explained that the root cause of all of my symptoms was excessive stress.

My further research revealed that according to Dr. Michael Lam, "one of the most common causes of postural orthostatic tachycardia syndrome is adrenal fatigue. In advanced stages of adrenal fatigue, the body's autonomic nervous system is in disarray. This can lead to sympathetic overtone, with POTS symptoms. Unfortunately, this is often missed by most physicians, as they are under-educated about adrenal fatigue and thus not on alert for these symptoms."[1] For a medical doctor both to have insufficient knowledge about adrenal issues and to make an inaccurate diagnosis is totally outrageous. This results in misdiagnoses and suggestions for incorrect treatments, which may be dangerous and risky.

My research on thyroid storm revealed that it is a life-threatening health condition that is most often associated with untreated hyperthyroidism. However, this association was not the case for me because I did not have hyperthyroidism. Thyroid storm speeds metabolic processes in the body. During a thyroid storm, an individual's heart rate, blood pressure, and body temperature can soar to dangerously high levels. I experienced the elevated heart rate and blood pressure, but my body temperature remained normal.

Finally, it all made sense! I had an advanced stage of adrenal fatigue that caused POTS and the thyroid storm symptoms. My holistic doctor instructed me to stop all medications immediately and prescribed both homeopathic remedies and herbal medicines. Within one week of following this advice and treatment plan, I no longer had to use a wheelchair to get around. I was able to stand for long periods and to walk again. Another miracle had taken place in my life. Traditional medicine doctors had led me to believe that I would never be able to stand or walk again. Dr. W. helped me tremendously, and I am very thankful that I sought his help. I had overcome a huge obstacle.

Although I was on my way to recovery, I had not yet reached optimal health. My mother, who came to visit me from Israel, brought with her an Israeli magazine. While I was reading it, I came across an advertisement for Hippocrates Health Institute in West Palm Beach, Florida. I looked into the institute, did some additional research, and then decided to take part in their life transformation program.

The results I attained after participating in a three-week program at the institute certainly indicated that all the conventional medical doctors I had consulted were wrong. On the advice of the Hippocrates Health Institute's program, I used a natural and healthy regimen, adopting a specific diet and other natural modalities. The healing required a lot of patience, strength, and commitment, but I was beyond letting anything stand in the way of regaining my health. I was ready to do whatever it took.

With my daughter Michelle in Sedona, AZ. before taking part in the transformation program at the Hippocrates Health Institute.

I am so grateful and I consider myself very lucky to have made the decision to participate in the transformation program at Hippocrates Health Institute. It was not an easy or quick recovery, but with persistence and inner strength, I not only made a full recovery but also reached optimal health. I returned home from the institute to celebrate my daughter's twelfth birthday. I knew with all my heart that my restored health was the best gift I could give her.

I cannot begin to express how happy and thankful I was. Imagine how amazing it felt to finally regain my health, to function independently after almost a year of being bedridden, to be given a second chance at a healthy, active life. I made courageous and drastic decisions and changes in all areas of my life. I assure you that if I had not made those changes, I would not be here to tell the story. I am blessed that because of these marked changes, the condition was temporary. Beyond the alterations in my diet, many other changes in my lifestyle—all of which I describe in this book—helped me to heal myself. The advice I offer in this book may help others with adrenal issues or POTS, but it can also be applied to many other health conditions and diseases.

I must admit that the year I was "out of commission," was the best year of my life in terms of developing self-awareness and self-reflection. I learned to channel the appropriate amount of energy in the right direction. I also assessed my life and reached the conclusion that the body has the ability to heal itself. Instead of having the determination to change my situation, I could have chosen to complain, to feel like a victim. However, as the saying goes, "When life gives you lemons, make lemonade." I decided to be optimistic and empowered and to empower others who are experiencing similar health challenges.

That is why I decided to write and share how I healed from adrenal fatigue and exhaustion, repaired the damage that was caused by excess stress, and brought myself back to optimal health. This book will detail the changes that I applied to my lifestyle to get my body back in balance, elaborating on how all aspects of health are interconnected with one another and are necessary to reach optimal health. As stated previously, I am not a doctor, but I have extensive knowledge of nutrition and natural modalities. Throughout the years, I attended hundreds of lectures, seminars, and workshops taught by medical professionals. I conducted countless interviews with people who had health issues and were able to heal themselves using natural modalities. I am now thrilled to share all of this knowledge along with my thirty years of intense research on healthy lifestyles condensed into a single book.

This book does not discuss low-fat or drastic diets for the purpose of weight loss. Instead, it expands beyond that goal to describe various healthy diets that establish nutritional needs, with weight loss as a side benefit. I share my knowledge and experience regarding all the diets and healing modalities that I have followed, describing what worked for me. You can apply any of these changes as I describe or adjust them to fit your body and lifestyle, although the lifestyle changes described herein are best monitored by a health care practitioner. I will review and summarize healthy diet types, describing the controversies surrounding each and explaining their benefits and drawbacks.

I will make recommendations on which foods and beverages to consume and which vitamins and supplements to take to keep your body functioning at an optimal level. I also discuss the benefits of detoxification or cleansing and provide detailed protocols. At the core of this book is the message that stress plays a critical and damaging role in our lives. Thus, I describe how to keep its detrimental effects on our bodies to a minimum through the use of mind control and other relaxation techniques and healing methods. I will cover the topic of physical activity, discussing various types of yoga and other exercise. Finally, I discuss the benefits and drawbacks of the various holistic healing modalities versus conventional medicine techniques, touching on diagnostic tools as well as treatments.

The purpose of this book is to share my knowledge, conclusions, opinions, and views on healthful living. I have successfully applied this knowledge to my own situation, and I have friends and family who have applied it to themselves with excellent results. Perhaps the key take away lessons are that (1) through the all-important mind-body-spirit connections, stress plays an enormous role in our lives, so we must learn to keep it under control; and (2) we can be our own doctor if we listen to the body's signals. Let's begin your journey to optimal health.

With my daughter Michelle in Sedona, AZ. prior to starting detox.

"Skip the diet, just eat healthy!"

– Unknown.

Taly Cotler.
The Stressed Vegan

Chapter 2

Diet Types

This chapter reviews and summarizes healthy diet types as viewed through the lens of my insights, knowledge, and experience, providing their benefits and limitations and pointing out the diet that I used to regain optimal health. When I use the term "diet" in this book, I am not referring to a weight loss plan. Instead, I am using the word in a more traditional sense, meaning the types of foods and beverages people consume, which can lead to weight loss but as a side benefit. This book offers neither a quick fix nor a weight loss diet per se but will reveal options in which you select one or a combination of a few diets that are most suitable to your body and lifestyle.

No matter which diet you choose, be sure to include not only good sources of protein, fat, and carbohydrates (which will be discussed in detail later) but also the correct percentages of each based on the Recommended Dietary Allowance or RDA. Some popular low carbohydrates diets, such as the Atkins or the ketogenic diet, include a high intake of protein and may consist of more fat than that allowed by the RDA. Therefore, exercise caution and choose your protein sources wisely to maintain the RDAs. As with most life choices, common sense prevails when selecting your food.

The types of diets that I consider healthy are described below and include vegetarian, vegan, raw vegan, blood type, Mediterranean, gluten-free, and paleo diets.

Some well-known vegetarian diets

People typically think that vegetarian diets include vegetables, fruits, eggs, dairy products, grains, and beans but exclude meat, poultry, and fish. Despite this broad general definition, vegetarian diets vary in the foods they include and exclude. Often vegetarian diets include high amounts of carbohydrates; however, consider limiting the amount and selecting high-quality carbohydrates. For examples of low and high quality carbohydrates, please refer to chapter 3.

The following is a brief overview of the most widely known types of vegetarian diets.

- Lacto-vegetarian: Allows dairy products, such as, milk, cheese, yogurt, and butter but excludes meat, fish, poultry, and eggs.
- Ovo-vegetarian: Allows eggs but excludes meat, poultry, seafood, and dairy products.
- Lacto-ovo vegetarian: Allows dairy products and eggs but excludes meat, fish, and poultry.
- Pescatarian: Allows fish but excludes meat, poultry, dairy products, and eggs. This diet is similar to the traditional Mediterranean diet in that both are plant-based, with fish serving as a primary animal protein.
- Pollotarian: Allows poultry but excludes meat, dairy products, and fish.
- Semi-vegetarian, also called flexitarian: Primarily a plant-based diet but includes meat, dairy products, eggs, poultry, and fish on occasion or in small quantities.
- Vegan: Includes mainly fruits and vegetables, grains, legumes, nuts, seeds, and soy, all of which can be either cooked or raw. It excludes eggs, dairy products, meat, poultry, and fish as well as foods that contain these products.

- Raw vegan also known as raw food: This plant-based diet includes mainly fruits, vegetables, seeds, nuts, grains, and legumes. All foods are eaten raw, that is, nothing is cooked. Grains and legumes are sprouted, and some foods are dehydrated. It excludes meat, poultry, fish, dairy products, and eggs.

- Blood type: Created by naturopath Peter J. D'Adamo, N.D. This diet is based on an individual's blood type. Although the diet is not supported by scientific evidence, it is highly recommended by many nutritionists and holistic medicine practitioners.

- Mediterranean: Emphasizes plant-based foods such as fruits, vegetables, whole grains, legumes, and nuts. It replaces butter with healthy fats, such as olive oil, and uses herbs and spices instead of salt to flavor foods. Red meat is limited to no more than a few times a month, whereas fish and chicken are on the menu a few times a week. People who follow the Mediterranean diet appear to have a longer life expectancy and lower rates of chronic diseases than do adults who do not adhere to the diet. Indeed, the Dietary Guidelines for Americans point to the Mediterranean diet as an example of a healthy-eating plan.[2]

- Gluten-free: Includes all foods but excludes those containing the protein gluten, which is mainly found in grains.

- Paleo: Includes fruits, vegetables, lean meats, seafood, nuts, seeds, and healthy fats but excludes dairy products, grains, processed foods and sugars, legumes, starches, and alcohol. For examples of healthy fats, please refer to chapter 3.

All the aforementioned diets offer health benefits but include a few drawbacks that required consideration when selecting a diet. This book focuses and elaborates on the blood type, vegan, raw vegan, and gluten-free diets. I mostly follow these diets and believe that they are especially important for people who are 40 years or older to incorporate into their lifestyles.

"Aging causes many people to experience problems with digestion." According to Life Extension, "It is estimated that after age 40 there is an approximate decrease of 20%-30% in the body's ability to produce enzymes. The use of specific enzymes can help improve the efficiency of digestion. Enzymes can be used to enhance the proper breakdown of foods in order to more properly digest, absorb, and utilize nutrients."[3]

Wouldn't it be wise to make changes to our diets that accommodate this slowing in digestion at that age?

Healthy diets I recommend for people 40 years or older
Blood type diet

Below is a general outline of the foods recommended for people by blood type. However, for details, please refer to Dr. D'Adamo's book *Eat Right 4 Your Type.*

- Type A: A meat-free diet based mainly on fruits, vegetables, beans, legumes, and grains.
- Type B: Includes meat, fish, eggs, and low-fat dairy. However, avoids corn, chicken, wheat, lentils, tomatoes, and peanuts.
- Type O: A high-protein diet heavy on meat and vegetables and light on grains and dairy products.
- Type AB: Foods to focus on include tofu, seafood, dairy, and green vegetables.

Dr. D'Adamo claims that "the foods you eat react chemically with your blood type. If you follow a diet designed for your blood type, your body will digest food more efficient, you will lose weight, have more energy and help prevent disease." He goes on to state that "when a blood type diet is followed, the result is high performance, mental clarity, greater vitality and increased longevity."[4]

However, no matter what your blood type is, you should follow the guidelines issued by The American Heart Association (AHA) for a low-fat, low-sugar, and low-sodium diet.[5]

If you have type O, the blood type diet proponents suggest consuming a high percentage of meat. Because of this heavy consumption of meat, use common sense when selecting your foods. Quality and lean meats should be eaten and in small quantities. Also keep in mind that meat from organic and grass-fed animals is a much better choice than non-organic.

If you are blood type B, for example, avoid eating chicken. If you do eat chicken, it may be toxic to your body and cause you to gain weight. However, eliminating chicken from your diet will create a less toxic environment and cause you to lose weight.

The blood type diet is important to follow especially as you age. Experiment with this diet and see if it works for you.

Raw vegan diet

Ann Wigmore, who was a holistic health practitioner and raw food advocate, founded Hippocrates Health Institute. The original Hippocrates Health Institute was in Boston, Massachusetts, and was later moved to West Palm Beach, Florida. Ann Wigmore believed in

Hippocrates' teaching that our food should be our medicine and our medicine should be our food.

In one of the lectures I attended by Dr. Brian Clement at Hippocrates Health Institute in West Palm Beach, Florida, he said that "foods that are cooked above temperatures of 104–120 °F have lost much of their nutritional value and are less healthy or even harmful to the body." He and others believe that heating food generates toxic materials and destroys the natural enzymes found in raw living foods that are critical for building proteins and rebuilding the body.

After completing the three-week program at the institute, I went home and applied the knowledge that I had acquired. The transition from a vegetarian to a raw vegan diet was not difficult for me. I merely had to give up dairy, eggs, and cooked foods, none of which I cared for all that much anyway. But even if the transition had been difficult, I would have felt that it was worth the benefits. I enjoyed watching my body gradually getting better, gaining more energy every day. I continued the protocol on my own for a year. Yes, it took a strong will and commitment, but the results were worth it. Other people I know who have healed themselves by adhering to the raw vegan diet also had to be entirely committed to the program to see their positive results. They could not cheat while they were healing. If they did, the disease would return. It takes a lot of persistence and commitment to make such a major change in your diet and lifestyle, but if it could save your life, wouldn't it be worth it to you too? Once the disease has been overcome, then there is room for flexibility in your diet choices. For myself, I stayed with the raw vegan diet for a year and then found I could transition to a more flexible vegan diet and still maintain my optimal health. So take heart! What some people might view as a rigid protocol is a commitment to life but may not be a life-long commitment.

You may wonder how the raw vegan diet works. Acidic bodies are unhealthy bodies, whereas alkaline bodies are healthier. When the body is acidic, it creates an environment in which illness, bacteria, and yeast thrive. To get the pH level of the body back into balance (from acidic to alkaline), it is highly recommended to incorporate a detoxification program with the raw vegan diet. It seems miraculous to be able to reverse many degenerative diseases by adapting to this way of life. I know people who were able to heal themselves from cancer or other diseases, including diabetes or thyroid issues. Our bodies are amazing and very powerful—they can heal themselves if they get the help they need. This way of life also saved my life, so I have first-hand experience. I healed myself from adrenal exhaustion and POTS using this approach, and I have been able to maintain good health. Today I am thrilled to say that I never felt as good or energetic in my life; I feel at least twenty years younger than my age. The goal of the diet is to ensure that your body is as alkaline as possible through the food you choose to eat. However, other aspects of wellness are important as well, and I will cover them all in the upcoming chapters.

Keep in mind that the changes in diet and lifestyle I recommend should always be initiated and maintained after consulting with your doctor. Some people cannot sustain a raw vegan diet and end up going back to eating a non-healthy diet, returning to the vicious cycle of getting sick again. If it heals you and makes you feel good, why not try adapting to a healthier way of life? I realize that the transition for carnivores to a raw vegan diet will be more difficult than my transition was. It may also take longer for such people to become used to this new way of life and to notice a significant improvement in their health. But those who have stuck with the diet found improvements in their sleep, mood, ability to focus, sharpness of mind, and energy levels. For those people who were pretty sick when they switched, the differences and benefits (e.g., weight loss and lower blood pressure and cholesterol levels) were so amazing to them that most have yet to go back to their old eating habits.

Many people following the raw vegan diet include gluten, but a great many do not. After the detoxification process, many people adopt a plant-based diet, such as a vegan or vegetarian diet. It is important to eat fresh and organic raw vegetables and fruits to increase the nutrient level in the food you consume. In my opinion, the raw vegan diet along with the detox process is very powerful in healing many major illnesses, including cancer. In some cases, however, an illness may have advanced too far for the raw vegan diet to be of much help. In addition, genetic factors may play an important role in some diseases; however, "genes do not determine disease on their own. Genes function only by being activated, or expressed, and nutrition plays a critical role in determining which genes, good and bad, are expressed."[6]

Vegan diet

The vegan diet is a plant-based diet that is high in fruits and vegetables. This diet includes grains, legumes, nuts, seeds, and soy, all of which can be either cooked or raw. It excludes meat, poultry, fish, eggs, and dairy products. The vegan diet can be highly nutritious because it is low in saturated fats and rich in nutrients. Eating vegan is known to be a healthier way of life because it lowers the risks of many major illnesses. Some people mistakenly think that vegan food is tasteless and boring. However, add spices and herbs and it becomes as delicious as meat dishes but with healthier ingredients. Experiment with different recipes until you find the ones you fall in love with. For example, just as there are numerous ways to make a hamburger, so too are there many ways to make a vegan burger. Some may be more suited to your palate and have a texture you like better than others. So do not give up the first time you try a vegan burger if you don't like it. Websites with tons of free vegan recipes are just a mouse click away.

Being vegan works for many people with different blood types, but it may be challenging for some people who are blood type O. As mentioned above, people with blood type O may need to eat some red meat to keep their bodies in balance. Although most people with type O blood require meat in their diet, some manage to stay healthy by eating a vegan diet.

There are two additional issues that are important to be aware of when eating a vegan diet. The first is maintaining normal cholesterol levels. A certain level of cholesterol is required in the body to perform specific functions normally, especially to keep hormones in balance. There is no doubt that a relationship exists between cholesterol and hormone production in the body.[7] People who eat vegan diets tend to have cholesterol levels that run low. Thus, serum cholesterol levels should be checked occasionally by a health care professional through a blood test to ensure that they remain within the normal range.

The second issue that vegans need to be aware of is their vitamin B12 levels. This vitamin has a key role in supporting normal functioning of the brain and the nervous system. Food sources of B12 are mainly red meat, so it is highly recommended for vegetarians and vegans to supplement with B12. Either the sublingual form of B12 or B12 shots could be considered.

Gluten-free diet

The gluten-free diet excludes the protein gluten, which is found mainly in grains, such as wheat, barley, rye, and spelt. Gluten helps foods maintain their shape, acting as glue that holds food together. Gluten can be found in numerous types of foods, even ones in which it may not be expected, such as soy sauce. A gluten-free diet is primarily used to treat celiac disease, which causes inflammation in the small intestines.[8] However, according to my research, gluten can cause inflammation anywhere in the body and is very detrimental to many organs and systems, especially the digestive system. It is advisable for people who experience issues with their endocrine system, specifically the thyroid gland, to avoid gluten because of its inflammatory effect. Gluten may also cause leaky gut syndrome, a condition in which the lining of the small intestine is damaged so that toxic waste leaks into the bloodstream.[9] Those who are gluten-free can still enjoy a healthy diet filled with fruits, vegetables, meats, poultry, fish, beans, legumes, and most dairy products. Such ingredients are naturally gluten-free and safe for individuals who do not have allergies to these particular food groups.

Taking all the information described in this chapter into consideration, I would suggest paying attention to the signals your body is sending and using common sense when selecting your diet type and food. A great idea to help with this is to keep a food journal and observe how you feel after eating certain foods. If a certain food makes you feel good, keep it in your diet, and if it does not, avoid eating it. What may work for one person, may not work for another. Also, what may work for you at age 20, may not work for you at age 50 because our bodies constantly change. In conclusion, eat what works best for you, as long as it makes you feel good, healthy, and energetic. For more information about any of the topics mentioned in this chapter, please refer to the resources section under "Diet Types."

- Eat food as medicine.
- Pay attention to the signals your body is sending.
- keep a food journal to determine what foods are best for you.

Taly Cotler,
The Stressed Vegan

"Let food be thy medicine and medicine be thy food."

– Hippocrates

Taly Cotler,
The Stressed Vegan

CHAPTER 3

Recommended Foods and Beverages

In terms of my diet and the foods I eat, I have always preferred quality to quantity. There is no doubt that it is better to consume a diet dense with nutrients rather than one dense with calories. It makes sense that when we eat nutrient-dense foods, our bodies are satisfied with small meals because they receive all the nutrition that they require. By contrast, when we eat poor quality foods dense with sugar, fat, and other bad ingredients, our bodies crave nutrients, and therefore we tend to overeat. However, if we eat what are called superfoods, we support our bodies with all that they need to function at an optimal level. We can eat either foods that heal and maintain our health or foods that make us sick and cause diseases in our bodies. The choice is ours. Choose wisely because not all foods are good for our health.

When I was sick, I committed myself to the 3-week program at Hippocrates Health Institute in West Palm Beach, Florida. I ate primarily vegetables, sprouts, legumes, seeds, and grains. I also juiced but strictly avoided all fruits and sugar. After I completed the program, I continued with a raw vegan diet for a year but incorporated a variety of fruits. To maintain my optimal health, I now eat a mostly gluten-free vegan diet but I also eat for my blood type. For me, five small meals per day work best. I feel more energetic eating this way rather than consuming three large meals. The digestive system does not have to work as hard when the amount is smaller, leaving more energy for other activities. I am also convinced that this helps to prevent the return of adrenal fatigue.

You may be thinking that my diet would be too rigid for you to adopt. But there is an abundance of wonderful options available now, as more people are starting to realize the benefits of diets loaded with vegetables and fruits and supply of recipes are beginning to meet the demand. I also admit that I am not as strict about my diet now as I had been during the first year after I completed the 3-week program at the institute. I believe that once you have achieved your optimal health, there is room for some flexibility.

Our diets are composed of three macronutrients: carbohydrates, protein, and fat. I next elaborate on these macronutrients as well as discuss other foods, organic foods, water, and other beverages.

Carbohydrates

Not all carbohydrates are equal, especially when it comes to their effects on cholesterol: some raise cholesterol, whereas others lower it. They are present in varying amounts in breads, cereals, grains, milk, yogurt, fruits, vegetables, and foods that contain added sugars. All carbohydrates are converted into glucose, which is also known as blood sugar, in the body, which can be used immediately for energy or stored for later use. Research suggests that both the quantity and type of carbohydrates consumed can affect cholesterol.[10]

Some common sources of simple carbohydrates that act like simple sugars in the body and provide mostly empty calories include white bread, white pasta, white rice, and potatoes. They are also found in processed and refined sugars, including candy, table sugar, syrups, and soft drinks as well as in fresh fruit and dairy products. When in doubt, avoid white, starchy foods. Instead, select non-refined, complex carbohydrates, which are considered "good carbs" and are far wiser choices. The best complex carbohydrates come from whole grains, vegetables, fruits, beans, legumes, nuts, and seeds. Whole wheat, whole grain, or gluten-free bread is a much bet-ter choice than white bread; sprouted wheat bread is even healthier because it is substantially easier to digest, but it does contain gluten. Whole wheat or gluten-free pasta is a better choice than white pasta. Brown rice is definitely more nutritious than white rice, and red potatoes or sweet potatoes are healthier than white potatoes. These choices are all superior for digestion and provide the body with more nutrients and are wiser sources of energy than simple carbohydrates.

It is also important to eat complex carbohydrates with a low glycemic index because this is a measure of how blood glucose levels are affected. Carbohydrates with a low glycemic index value (55 or less) are more slowly digested, absorbed, and metabolized and thus cause a lower and slower increase in blood glucose and insulin levels.

Sugar (simple carbs)

Many foods, for example, pasta, white potatoes, ketchup, syrup, and milk, contain high levels of white sugar. Excessive white sugar is harmful to your health and contains the least amount of nutrients. In terms of food, sugar is the number one cause of aging, and it has a significant negative effect on our bodies, especially our skin. I have read that every time you eat sugar, you gain a wrinkle.[11]

High consumption of sugar is especially detrimental to the bones, brain, and endocrine system although it also negatively affects the rest of the body. Sugar is one of the worst foods to consume because it elevates cholesterol and blood sugar levels, increasing the odds of diabetes or heart attack. It not only spikes your insulin, it also triggers inflammation, which makes us store belly fat and blocks our ability to feel full.

If you tend to consume high levels of sugar, try eating it with fiber, protein, and fat to lower the damage it causes the body. Of course, even better would be to totally eliminate it from your diet. Although there are several alternatives to white sugar, including brown sugar or artificial sweeteners, they may also have some risks.

Research has shown that stevia (extracted from the plant species *Stevia rebaudiana*) is a good alternative, especially for people with diabetes, and it is also known to regulate hypertension.[12] Stevia is available in many forms. The most popular is a white extract powder, but you can also buy stevia as dried leaves, liquid extract, small pellets, or in a granular form in small packets to sweeten your foods or beverages. Rather than consume white or brown sugar, I prefer stevia, agave (syrup from the agave plant), or Lakanto (from monk fruit).

Protein

Meats

Red meat provides high amounts of protein, which helps build bones and muscles. It also supplies iron and vitamin B12 to help make DNA and keep nerve and red blood cells healthy. In addition, red meat contains zinc, a mineral that keeps the immune system working properly. Chicken, fish, and organic versions of any meat may seem a better choice than red meat, but those selections are not as safe as they seem. Organic and grass-fed animals are a wiser choice than non-organic. For individuals with type O blood, selecting bison, also referred to as buffalo, which contains fewer calories and less fat than other meats, is the better choice.

Despite these apparent benefits, there are many health risks associated with eating red meat. Some red meats are high in saturated fat, which raises blood cholesterol. High levels of low-density lipoprotein (LDL) cholesterol increase the risk of heart disease and diabetes. Processed meats, especially hot dogs and sausage, contain carcinogens that increase the odds of cancer. All animals providing meat may have been injected with artificial hormones and antibiotics, which are then transferred to the body of the consumer. In addition, meat carries the highest risk of food-borne illness. A vast array of studies from top universities and independent researchers has found that eating meat from chickens, cows, and other animals promotes many forms of cancer.[13] There is no doubt that there is a connection between meat consumption and cancer risk. The risks associated with eating red meat definitely outweigh the benefits; therefore, it is wise to cut down or eliminate your meat consumption.

Meat, dairy products, and eggs all contain cholesterol and saturated fat and contribute to America's top killers: heart attack, stroke, diabetes, and various types of cancer. They also contain hormones that can cause hormonal imbalances in our bodies.[14]

Seafood

Fish contains high amounts of protein and a wide variety of vitamins and minerals, including vitamins A and D, phosphorus, magnesium, and selenium. Research shows that omega-3 fatty acids, found abundantly in seafood, have health benefits, including protection against heart disease and stroke as well as improved infant brain development.

Current advice from the US government and health organizations recommends eating two seafood meals each week. Scientists from the US government and universities and health care professionals have all concluded that for most people, the overall benefits of this level of seafood consumption outweigh the potential food safety risks.[15]

Food-borne illnesses caused by microorganisms or naturally occurring toxins are the primary food safety risks associated with seafood, similar to other perishable foods. Illness is usually associated with improper harvesting, handling, storage, or preparation. Seafood products that are consumed raw or partially cooked present the highest risk.[16]

Other risks associated with environmental contaminants could be a concern for some individuals, especially those who catch and eat their own fish or shellfish from lakes or rivers that are contaminated by environmental pollutants. Fish products have been shown to contain various amounts of heavy metals, particularly mercury, and fat-soluble pollutants from water pollution. Species of fish that are long-lived and high on the food chain, such as tuna, shark, swordfish, king mackerel, and tilefish, contain higher concentrations of mercury than those lower on the food chain. Mercury is a highly toxic metal and is dangerous to humans because of its ability to damage the central nervous system and to have a strong effect on the brain, among other harmful effects. The presence of mercury in fish can be a particular health concern for women who are or may become pregnant, nursing mothers, and young children.

If you choose to include fish in your diet, I recommend wild-caught Alaskan salmon because it has low levels of heavy metals and does not contain the antibiotics and toxins seen in some farm-raised fish.[17]

Eggs

Eggs are a very good source of inexpensive, high quality protein. More than half the protein of an egg is found in the white part, which also has lower amounts of fat and cholesterol than the yolk. The yolks are rich sources of selenium, vitamins D, B6, and B12, and minerals, such as zinc, iron, and copper. However, many eggs contain hormones and antibiotics, which can lead to several health issues. The yolk, although containing important nutrients, is also high in cholesterol. Therefore it is recommended to eat no more than three eggs per week, especially if your cholesterol tends to run high. Boiling rather than frying eggs is a healthier option.[18]

Eating eggs measurably increases the risk of developing type 2 diabetes. A recent study found that eating three to five eggs per week doubled the chances of becoming diabetic, and individuals eating five or more eggs per week had three times the risk of this deadly disease.[19]

According to the Centers for Disease Control and Prevention (CDC), salmonella bacteria are frequently found on the outside as well as on the inside of eggs. It is not recommended to consume raw or undercooked eggs because of the risk of contracting salmonella. If you choose to eat eggs, I recommend buying "free range" or "cage-free" brands and organic eggs that are free of hormones and antibiotics.

Dairy

Consuming dairy products provides health benefits, especially improved bone health. Foods in the dairy group provide nutrients that are vital for the health and maintenance of your body. These nutrients include calcium, potassium, vitamin D, and protein. However, dairy products, including cheese, ice cream, milk, butter, and yogurt, contribute significant amounts of cholesterol and saturated fat to the diet. Diets high in fat and especially in saturated fat can increase the risk of heart disease and can cause other serious health problems. Some people appear to be lactose intolerant, but often the same symptoms are more likely caused by difficulty digesting the protein casein.[20]

Casein is the main protein found in milk and is also used in many food products as a binding agent. Dr. Colin Campbell conducted comprehensive studies on the link between casein and cancer and found that casein substantially increases the risk of cancer, especially breast and prostate cancers. Other research has shown that our bodies cannot easily digest dairy products. In addition, dairy products contain high levels of hormones and antibiotics.[21]

If you do not want to give up dairy products, especially cheese, I recommend selecting goat or sheep cheeses (particularly manchego cheese, from the manchego breed of sheep) that are made from raw rather than pasteurized milk. These types of cheeses are much easier to digest than those made from cow's milk although they may be a bit pricey.

Vegan protein

Vegetarians and vegans glean protein from lentils, beans, grains, nuts, seeds (e.g., sunflower, pumpkin, hemp, and chia seeds), and vegetables. Pea protein powder and soy products, such as tofu, edamame, tempeh, miso, and soybeans, are rich in protein and other important nutrients. Although soy-based foods are good alternatives to red meat and make a valuable contribution to overall healthy diet, the consumption of soy is controversial. Many researchers claim that soy food consumption may be associated with elevated estrogen, and as a result it may increase the risk of breast and endometrial cancers. However, other studies indicate otherwise. Soy food consumption may also cause hormonal imbalances as well as interrupt the functioning of the thyroid gland. I suggest eating soy products in moderation and selecting the organic non-genetically modified organism (non-GMO) versions.

Vegetables

Eat an assortment of vegetables, preferably organic and raw. Vegetables are an important part of the diet because they are rich in vitamins and minerals, which help you feel healthy and energized. When vegetables—or for that matter when any foods—are cooked, the nutritional value and enzyme levels decrease.

Fruits

Eat a wide variety of fruits that have a low glycemic index. However, certain fruits should not be mixed with others. For example, those that are sweet (such as bananas and grapes) can be eaten together, and those that are acidic (such as oranges and kiwis) can be eaten together, but sweet and acidic fruits should not be eaten at the same time to avoid slowing digestion. Fruit should be eaten on an empty stomach or at the beginning of the meal, never at the end of the meal.

According to my research, when fruit is eaten at the end of the meal, the sugar in the fruit causes fermentation in the body and most of the nutrients of the fruit are lost. By contrast, fruit eaten as a snack or the beginning of the meal will play a major role in detoxifying your system, supplying you with a great deal of nutrients.[22]

Fats

A small amount of fat is an essential part of a healthy and balanced diet and helps the body absorb vitamins A, D, and E. These vitamins are fat-soluble, meaning they can only be absorbed with the help of fats. The human body can make most fats, with the exception of omega-3 and omega-6, as mentioned previously. If you do not include enough of the omega fatty acids in your diet, you may experience symptoms of dry and flaky skin as well as dry and brittle hair. Keep in mind that all foods contain a mixture of fats. Even "healthy" foods, such as chicken, fish, nuts, and oils, contribute some saturated fat to the diet although these foods are much lower in saturated fat than beef, cheese, and ice cream. Eating saturated fat does not increase blood triglyceride levels as much as eating a diet high in carbohydrates. Elevated blood triglycerides cause inflammation and plaque buildup in the arteries, increasing the risk of heart disease. Small, dense LDL cholesterol particles also increase heart disease risk.[23]

Examples of good choices of healthy fats are olive oil and coconut oil, whereas examples of poor choices of fat are butter, margarine, and canola oil.

Most of us have been led to believe that cholesterol is the culprit behind rising rates of heart disease. We have been told that lowering fat and cholesterol and using vegetable oil and other substitutes in our diet will protect us from heart disease. Although there is more evidence available that suggests that cholesterol protects us from heart disease and stroke, I think it is still important to keep it within normal levels, not too high though. However, your body is incapable

of making hormones without cholesterol, so you would not want it on the low side either.[24]

Trans fat

Trans fat, also known as trans fatty acids, are unhealthy substances made through the chemical hydrogenation of oils. Hydrogenation solidifies liquid oils and increases their shelf life and the flavor stability of oils and foods that contain them. Trans fat is found in vegetable shortening and in some margarines, crackers, cake and cookie mixes, doughnuts, snack foods, french fries, and other foods. "Trans fats wreak havoc with the body's ability to regulate cholesterol. In the hierarchy of fats, the polyunsaturated fats, which are found in vegetables, are the good kind; they lower your cholesterol. Saturated fats have been condemned as the bad kind. But trans fats are far worse. They drive up the LDL (bad) cholesterol, which markedly increases the risk of coronary artery heart disease and stroke."[25]

<u>Organic Foods</u>

"Organic agriculture is an ecological production management system that promotes and enhances biodiversity, biological cycles and soil biological activity. It is based on minimal use of off-farm inputs and on management practices that restore, maintain and enhance ecological harmony."[26] Essentially, this includes crops that are grown without the use of synthetic pesticides, artificial fertilizers, heavy metals, solvents, and biotechnology.

Organically grown foods have more nutrients than commercially grown foods because the soil is managed and nourished with sustainable practices using responsible standards.[27]

By using organic foods and avoiding harmful pesticides and fertilizers, people can increase their intake of phytochemicals (plant-derived vitamins and antioxidants) while reducing their exposure to the antibiotics and pesticides that research has linked to damaging results in public health. Organic foods are generally much healthier than conventional foods because they contain sustainably higher nutrients of vitamins, minerals, enzymes, and micronutrients. The higher nutritional values rely on the soil in which the food is grown and whether it meets the standard of sustainable practice. In comparison to conventional foods, organically grown foods contain higher concentrations of nutrients, and they taste better. By eating organic foods you also avoid GMO foods because certified organic food cannot be genetically modified in any way. In addition, if you consume certified organic animal products, you avoid hormones, antibiotics, and other drugs that exist in conventional meat and dairy.[28]

Beverages

It is well known that it is crucial to maintain a balance of fluids in the body. Water is the healthiest easily available beverage to keep your body working efficiently. Other good beverage choices are green tea and freshly squeezed vegetable or fruit juices. It is recommended to drink at least eight glasses of fluids daily to maintain normal body functions. Water is the best beverage to quench your thirst, and it offers many health benefits that I will detail next. However, green tea can help reduce the risk of cancer, heart disease, and cavities. Vegetable juice also offers many health benefits and plays a significant role in detoxification. Unsweetened cranberry juice is a good choice for a fruit juice. It is often recommended for drinking during long airline flights to boost the immune system. The health benefits of cranberry juice also include helping to fight colds and gum disease, avoid respiratory tract infections, and provide relief from urinary tract infections and kidney stones.[29]

Water

Your body is composed of about 60% water. Drinking water is essential to your health! This important nutrient is present in liquids, plain water, fruits, and other foods. All of these are essential on a daily basis to replace the large amounts of water lost each day. It is imperative to replenish the water lost to prevent dehydration. Fluid losses are accentuated in warmer climates and during strenuous exercise.[30] If you are thirsty, listen to your body, and drink water or other healthful beverages.

Water helps maintain normal body functions. It is important for digestion, absorption, circulation, creation of saliva, transportation of nutrients, and maintenance of body temperature. Drinking water can also help control calorie intake. Drinking enough fluids is important when exercising to replace fluids lost by sweating, and water helps energize muscles. Water keeps our skin looking good. Your skin contains plenty of water and functions as a protective barrier to prevent excess fluid loss. Water helps your kidneys do an amazing job of cleansing and ridding your body of toxins as long as your intake of fluids is adequate. If your fluid intake is too low, you may be at higher risk for kidney stones, especially in warm climates.[31]

There are many different types of filtered water, and it is definitely better to drink alkaline than acidic water. The pH level is a measure on a scale of zero to fourteen of how acidic or alkaline a substance is. A substance with a pH of 1 would be very acidic, and a substance with a pH of 14 would be very alkaline. As I explained in chapter 2, the more alkaline your body is, the healthier you are. Reverse osmosis is a water filtration system that uses a membrane to remove ions, molecules, and larger particles from drinking water. Reverse osmosis can remove many types of dissolved and suspended species from water, including bacteria. The pH of water filtered via reverse osmosis is approximately 4.0.[32]

Distilled water is water that has had many of its impurities removed through distillation. Distillation involves boiling the water and then condensing the steam into a clean container. Distilled water has a pH of about 6.0. Thus, distilled water is more alkaline than water that went through reverse osmosis filtration.[33] Regular tap water generally has a pH of 6 to 7, whereas alkaline water has a pH of 8 or 9.[34] Alkaline water goes through filtration, but tap water does not. Alkaline water is water that has been ionized, meaning that the pH level has been increased. This process also removes about 99% of the thousands of potential chemicals that may be in your tap water. Alkaline water ionizers are offered for home use or can be purchased at health food stores. I recommend drinking high quality alkaline water and other fluids to keep your body hydrated.

Beverages to avoid

Avoid trying to quench your thirst with soda, bottled fruit juices, and alcoholic beverages because those choices can be deceptively high in sugar and calories. At all costs, avoid energy drinks and limit your consumption of coffee because of their caffeine content. Eliminate all carbonated soft drinks from your diet. Common soft drinks, particularly colas (very low pH of 2.3), contain about 39 grams of sugar, and diet sodas contain artificial sweeteners, such as aspartame, that is very high in phenylalanine, which has detrimental effects on our health. Statistics show that Americans are drinking more soda than ever before. A typical twenty ounce soda contains anywhere between fifteen and eighteen teaspoons of sugar and about 240 calories.

Here's more information that may keep you from drinking a soda. Both regular and diet sodas are significant contributors to obesity. Anything that promotes weight gain also increases the risk of diabetes. Consumption of too many soft drinks puts you at increased risk of liver cirrhosis, similar to the increased risk faced by people with alcohol use disorder. Soda also dissolves tooth enamel and causes tooth decay. High consumption of sodas increases risk of heart disease and gout and possibly of kidney stones. Drinking soda has so many detrimental effects on your health that avoiding it all together is a smart decision.[35]

Some people like to drink alcohol, a glass of wine, beer, or a cocktail, in social gatherings because it makes it easier for them to meet, mingle, and enjoy themselves. Another reason people like to drink alcohol is its value as a relaxant. However, alcohol can have detrimental effects on your body. When you drink alcohol, it is absorbed into your bloodstream and affects every part of your body. In the long term, this can put your health at serious risk. Alcohol interferes with the functioning of the liver, brain, heart, and more. In my opinion, drinking in moderation could be wise, but eliminating alcohol from your diet may be even wiser. There are healthier options than drinking alcohol to promote relaxation. For more information about healthful relaxation methods, please refer to chapters 7, 8 and 9.

For more information about any of the topics mentioned in this chapter, please refer to the resources section under "Recommended Foods and Beverages."

- Eat five small meals per day.
- Stay away from refined foods.
- Limit your sugar intake.
- Eat fruit as a snack not as a dessert.
- Drink high quality purified water between meals.
- Never combine protein and carbohydrates at the same meal.

Taly Cotler,
The Stressed Vegan

"Good nutrition creates health in
all areas of our existence.
All parts are interconnected."

—T. Colin Campbell

CHAPTER 4

Vitamins and Supplements

The understanding that we must consume supplements or vitamins grew from the realization that the modern diet fails to supply the body with enough micronutrients to support optimal health.[36] Food alone may not provide sufficient micronutrients. Vitamin and mineral supplements can help prevent deficiencies that can contribute to chronic conditions. Numerous studies have shown the health benefits and effectiveness of supplementing nutrients missing in the diet.[37] Regardless of whether we get vitamins from our daily diet, from sunshine, or from store-bought supplements, they are vital to our health and the proper functioning of our bodies. Vitamin deficiencies lead to a wide range of health issues, spanning from anorexia to obesity, and include organ malfunction, depression, and others.

However, whether nutritional supplements are harmful is another story. All supplements are not created equal, and many of them are synthetic. Certain supplements contain fillers and chemicals, and capsules and soft gels are made of synthetic ingredients. Those chemicals and synthetic ingredients could have bad effects on your health.[38]

Whether vitamins and supplements are actually needed is controversial. In my opinion, most skeptics are conventional medicine practitioners who may feel threatened that there are healthier options than the medications they prescribe. I also believe that pharmaceutical companies may feel that the vitamin industry may affect their bottom line, and they may be intimidated by the field that is called alternative medicine. Many drug companies may claim that vitamins are a waste of money. Supplements are definitely a big industry; however, it is challenging to obtain all the necessary vitamins, minerals, and nutrients from food alone. We cannot eat enough food to provide us with all the nutrients that we need. So it is usually recommended to take nutritional supplements.[39]

It makes sense that someone whose diet is poor and lacking important nutrients and vitamins needs to take more supplements than someone who eats a healthy diet containing high levels of nutrients. However, even if your diet is very healthy, there is still a need to supplement it with good quality vitamins. The ideal situation is to eat a balanced diet that is rich in fruits and vegetables and to supplement that diet with the vitamins and minerals that your body needs to function at an optimal level. This is especially important given that food these days is mostly processed and lacking the essential nutrients that are necessary for the normal functioning of the body.

The remainder of this chapter answers some common questions about nutritional supplements.

<u>Which vitamins should be taken?</u>

I recommend a good quality multivitamin that contains probiotics, but I also encourage you to take additional probiotics separately. As we get older, we should take more probiotics, especially women over the age of 40.[40]

Probiotics are live bacteria and yeasts that are good for our health, especially the digestive and immune systems. Probiotics are often called "good" or "helpful" bacteria because they help maintain a healthy gut. Many integrative medicine practitioners recommend taking extra probiotics especially after a bad cold because that is when the immune system is weak and suppressed. Taking antibiotics kills both bad and good bacteria. Therefore, isn't it wise to supplement with probiotics that will replace the good bacteria that were killed by the antibiotics?

A good quality multivitamin formula should also contain digestive enzymes to support the digestive system. Digestive enzymes help the body absorb more nutrients and improve gut health. Depending on the quality of your digestion and your age, it may even be a good idea to supplement with additional digestive enzymes, especially if you eat a lot of cooked food that contains small amounts of enzymes. It is recommended to take both probiotics and digestive enzymes on an empty stomach prior to a meal.

In general, if you eat a healthy diet, a good multivitamin formula should be sufficient. However, if the formula does not have enough of a specific vitamin or mineral that you may need, it is a good idea to add that supplement to the multivitamin. For example, women who are older than 40 years should take calcium/magnesium supplements in addition to a multivitamin. In regards to vitamin D, other than getting it from foods that are rich in vitamin D or from supplements, you can make it by exposing your skin to the sun. Although vitamin D is important and can help minimize the chances of getting many illnesses, it is suggested to monitor the dosage and not to overdose on vitamin D because it can be toxic above certain levels.

While I was recovering, I supplemented my diet with vitamins C and B complex, magnesium, L-theanine, and phosphatidylserine. I also took adaptogenic herbs, including ashwagandha, rhodiola, and licorice root. Currently, to maintain my good health, I take a high-quality multivitamin, probiotics, digestive enzymes, vitamins B12, C, and D, calcium with magnesium, omega-3, and omega-6. To prevent the common cold or flu, neither of which I have experienced for many years now, every once in a while, I take an extra dose of vitamin C along with echinacea and goldenseal. Since I regained my health, I handle stress much better than before I became ill, but during times of very high stress, I will take vitamin B complex and the aforementioned adaptogenic herbs to support my adrenal glands.

I highly recommend asking your doctor to order blood tests that check for levels of micronutrients before taking any additional vitamins. The test measures the levels of specific vitamins, minerals, amino acids, and other nutrients in the blood. Such blood tests are usually pricey and most are not covered by medical insurance companies, but it is well worth the investment. Remember your health comes first! Once the results come back, a doctor can determine which vitamins or elements are missing in your body and recommend supplements to replenish them.

Which forms of vitamins are better?

Supplements come in many forms: tablets, capsules, liquid, powder, soft gels, and sublingual. Some are absorbed by the body better than others. The amount of vitamins taken is not as important as the amount that gets absorbed or assimilated in the body. A person can only gain the full benefit of nutritional supplements if they are fully absorbed. Multivitamins usually come in a tablet form, which is more potent but much harder to digest and absorb than capsules. Because vitamins in capsule form are much easier to absorb, the chances of getting most of the nutrients from the vitamins is increased. For example, in a comparison of tablets and capsules, to obtain approximately the same amount of vitamins/minerals as in a multivitamin, you would need four tablets versus six capsules. So if taking fewer pills is a consideration, tablets may be a good option. However, if you hope to absorb more nutrients, capsules will be the best choice. Soft gels are absorbed better than tablets and at about the same level as capsules. Vitamin E usually comes in soft gel form. Liquid and powder supplements get absorbed even better than capsules and soft gels. Supplements in powder form need to be mixed with water or another liquid when taken.

The sublingual form is a small tablet that is dissolved under the tongue and is easily absorbed. Vitamin B12 comes in this form and is absorbed much better than that provided in any other form. If you are concerned with maximizing absorption, I suggest taking vitamins in liquid or powder form. However, when traveling, it is much easier and more convenient to carry capsules, tablets, or soft gels, rather than liquids or powder.

An important point to keep in mind is that some nutrients, such as calcium and vitamin D, work in concert; they need one another's assistance to be fully absorbed.[41]

<u>Which brands are best?</u>

When it comes to vitamins, there are many companies offering different qualities to choose among. A rule of thumb is to ensure that there are no fillers or chemicals in the supplements. Also, if keeping kosher is a concern, vitamins that contain gelatin as part of their ingredients should be avoided. I like either New Chapter or Rainbow Light brands. They are plant-based supplements that contain no fillers or artificial ingredients. They are made out of whole foods and natural ingredients that are well absorbed in the body even in a tablet form. Most of the time, New Chapter and Rainbow Light supplements contain herbal formulas to support different organs or systems in the body. For example, some of the supplements contain digestive enzymes, probiotics, hormone support, stress support, or even liver support. These supplements can be taken with or without food. If a multivitamin that contains digestive enzymes is taken in addition to other enzymes supplements, it is wise not to exceed the daily allowance. The same rule applies to all other vitamins, minerals, or herbal medicines.

Although New Chapter and Rainbow Light are more expensive than other brands, they are well worth the investment. After all, vitamins are taken to support our health, so it is wise to take good quality supplements. We want to prevent them from having a detrimental effect on our bodies by avoiding the chemicals that some other supplements contain. I also like Life Extension and Garden of Life brands. Life Extension performs research and develops new formulas to treat various health issues. Many of Life Extension's supplements or formulas target and support specific organs or systems in our bodies that help us heal or slow down the aging process.

Herbal supplements may relieve everything from migraines to insomnia, but unless you are careful about where you obtain these supplements, you might be getting more than you bargained for—such as harmful chemicals or fillers. The Food and Drug Administration (FDA) does not regulate herbal supplements the same way it does food and drugs, so it is wise for consumers to do some research on their own and acquire herbs from reliable sources. Make sure you read labels carefully and stick with herbs organically produced in the United States and Europe. You may want to avoid herbs produced in China, India, or Mexico, where regulations are not as strict.

Other excellent brands that are sold only through health care professionals are Xymogen and Designs for Health. These and other brands have labels indicating that the products were produced according to quality standards. These labels are marked with COA (Certificate Of Analysis) or GMP (Good Manufacturing Practice) certificates.

Should vitamins be taken with or without food?

I suggest following the directions recommended on the label of the supplement or your doctor's instructions. Some vitamins are absorbed better with food and others are not. Amino acid supplements must be taken on an empty stomach or at least two hours after a meal and one hour before the next meal to maximize absorption.

Should vitamins/supplements be taken continuously?

I highly recommend taking vitamins for a few days per week and then stopping for a couple of days (e.g., five days on and two days off). Also, after taking vitamins for a few months, it is recommended to take a break for a few weeks just to rebalance the body and prevent vitamin overdose (e.g., take for two to three months and stop for two weeks or so). The same applies not only to vitamins or minerals but also to herbal medicine. For herbal medicines and amino acids, as a general rule, they should not be taken longer than three to four months. That is what I found works best for me. Also, prior to having a surgical procedure, certain vitamins should not be taken—consult your doctor for specific instructions. I also encourage you to consult your doctor or a nutritionist when it comes to which supplements you should take. Supplements and vitamins go through the liver to be absorbed. When too many vitamins are taken, it not only slows digestion but it also takes a toll on the liver. Therefore, it is very important to incorporate a break from supplements into your regimen.

Important supplemental vitamins/minerals/herbs

Vitamin A

This vitamin is important for growth and development, for the maintenance of the immune system, and for good vision.

Vitamin B complex

These essential nutrients help convert our food into fuel, allowing us to stay energized throughout the day. It is very important to take B complex during stressful times because stress depletes vitamin B in our bodies. Common symptoms of vitamin B deficiency include headache, insomnia, irritability, depression, or anemia.

Vitamin C

Vitamin C treats the common cold, boosts the immune system, lowers high blood pressure (hypertension), and maintains the elasticity of the skin among many other benefits.

Vitamin D

People with high serum cholesterol levels should increase their intake of vitamin D because high cholesterol is linked with low vitamin D. Also, vitamin D deficiency may be associated with heart disease and a higher risk of high blood pressure (hypertension).

Vitamin E

This vitamin improves vascular function and helps with high blood pressure in people with mild hypertension.

Calcium

Your body needs calcium to build and maintain strong bones. In addition, your heart, muscles, and nerves need calcium to function properly. Calcium also plays a key role in hormone and enzyme functions. Some studies show that it is more beneficial to take calcium along with magnesium for better absorption.

Magnesium

Magnesium has many benefits, including increasing energy, calming nerves, helping digestion, preventing migraine headaches, and helping to prevent osteoporosis among other benefits. Magnesium citrate is the easiest type of magnesium to absorb, and my least favorite type is magnesium carbonate because the carbonate may cause side effects.

Iron

Too little of this mineral is associated with anemia (a lack of red blood cells) and a weakened immune system. The health benefits of iron include the eradication of different causes of fatigue.

Zinc

This mineral is responsible for a number of different functions in the body. Zinc stimulates the immune system, helps treat the common cold, and aids wound healing.

Echinacea

This herb is believed to strengthen the immune system and reduce many of the symptoms associated with colds, flu, infections and some other illnesses.

Goldenseal

This herb is also used for the common cold and other upper respiratory tract infections. Some people use goldenseal for digestive issues. It is a very powerful herb with many healing properties. However, a University of Maryland Medical Center study showed that goldenseal's antibacterial action could destroy both good and harmful bacteria if used for an extended time. Therefore, it should not be used for a prolonged time.[42]

Omega-3 fatty acids

Studies have shown that higher levels of omega-3 fatty acids in the blood are strongly associated with improved cardiovascular health, whereas lower levels of omega-3 are linked to increased rates of hypertension and risk of heart attack. In addition to improving cardiovascular health, omega-3 improves rheumatoid arthritis, asthma, Alzheimer disease, depression, and vision. Omega-3 also reduces inflammation in the body. It can be found in fish, nuts (especially walnuts), and flaxseed or their oils as well as in vegetable oil and dark green leafy vegetables.

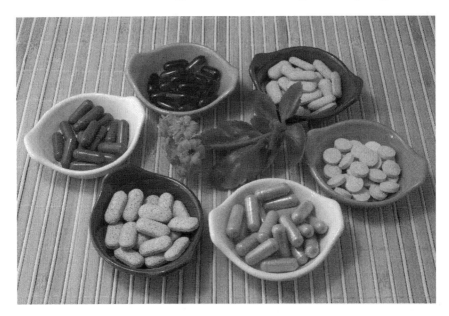

Omega-6 fatty acids

Both omega-3 and omega-6 are essential fatty acids that are neces-sary for human health. Something that is "essential" means that the body cannot make it, so we have to get it from food. Although both of these fatty acids can help fight inflammation, make sure that the ratio between omega 3 and omega 6 is balanced, with the level of omega 3 higher than that of omega 6. If that ratio is off, it increases the chances of inflammation in the body. I prefer alternating between fish oil and flax seed oil to maintain a balanced ratio and to increase the benefits of both types.

Amino acids

Amino acids are critical in muscle maintenance, tissue repair, immu-nity, and control of all your body's processes. When we consume protein, the body breaks it down to create a pool of single amino acids that our cells incorporate into new proteins as needed. Con-suming amino acids in the form of whole-food protein is preferable to taking them in through supplements. However, certain amino acid supplements can offer both health and fitness benefits.

Amino acids regulate almost all of the metabolic processes in the human body, and they are essential for a healthy body. Protein powders are wonderful sources of amino acids, especially for the branched-chain amino acids (BCAAs) that offer muscle-building benefits before or after a workout.

What are the muscle-building benefits of amino acids? Amino acids are the building blocks that make up protein. Your body puts them together like Legos to create muscle. The proteins through-out your body contain twenty different amino acids in various com-binations. The core of each amino acid is structurally similar, but each one also contains a portion that is different from every other one. These differences allow the amino acids, and the proteins they make up, to function in different ways. Supplements can include all the essential amino acids, a subset of these nutrients, or individual amino acids. Thus, there are many kinds of amino acid supplements that can be taken to help with various functions of the body.[43]

To summarize, make sure that you eat a healthy and a balanced diet and take nutritional supplements to support your health. Whether you take herbal medicines or any other vitamins or supplements, check with your doctor to ensure that there are no interactions with the medications you currently taking. Select good quality nutritional supplements to maximize absorption and health benefits. Remember to take supplements on a regular basis, but not continuously. It is important to take a break from them every now and then. Use capsules, powder, or liquid form supplements to maximize absorption and to get full benefits. Remember to follow the instructions on the label of the supplements as well as your doctor's instructions.

For more information about any of the topics mentioned in this chapter, please refer to the resources section under "Vitamins and Supplements."

- Consume good quality supplements.
- Capsules supplements are better absorbed than tablets.
- Don't take supplements continuously for long periods of time.

"Those who think they have no time for healthy eating will sooner or later have to find time for illness."

— Edward Stanley

CHAPTER 5

Detox/Cleansing

There is a direct relationship between the level of toxins in the body and how sick a person is, that is, the higher the toxin level, the sicker the person. Most people associate the detoxification process with deprivation; you eat very little and what little food you do eat is weird. This is untrue! There is no pain or suffering involved with detoxing. On the contrary, detoxing is an excellent way to jump start your health and reboot your metabolism. It is also a lot easier than you think. Detoxing can take from a few days to three weeks or longer depending on your health condition and the amount of toxicity you are experiencing. We get toxins from the food we eat, the air we breathe, the water we drink, the household cleaners we use, our personal care products, the environment, medications, stress, and even the electronics we use every day.[44] In addition, people who eat diets that include a lot of swordfish or tuna, which contain mercury, or those who have several dental amalgams fillings, may have toxin buildup.

Many people, although unaware, are being harmfully affected by bad diets that consist of red meat, lots of sugar and flour, dairy products, and junk foods. They are also probably unaware that they are being negatively affected by toxic free radicals that are being formed in their bodies. Stress hormones, negative emotions, anxiety, and emotional disturbances all create free radicals. You may be wondering how someone like me who ate a clean vegetarian diet of mostly organic foods, who did not drink or smoke or take medicines, and who was an avid exerciser could also have had an overload of toxins. I attribute my toxic overload associated with my illness to excessive, uncontrolled stress. When the body is under such stress, the adrenal glands release high amounts of cortisol, which can lead to a whopping amount of toxic free radicals that can cause not only inflammation but also an acidic environment, which as I explained in chapter 2 can lead to disease.

Nearly all diseases are due to a buildup of toxins in the body. Toxins cause detrimental effects, manifesting in many health issues, including cancer, cardiovascular disease, asthma, depression, autoimmune disorders, skin condition, and allergies. Examples of symptoms that may indicate an overload of toxins in the body are headaches, brain fog, fatigue, muscle aches, food allergies, overweight, hormone imbalance, and skin abnormalities. If you have any of these symptoms, you likely have a toxin overload. Although the body has a mechanism to deal with low levels

Vegetable juice such as: beet, cucumber, or carrot juice plays a significant role in detoxification.

of toxins, additional measures are necessary to deal with a toxin overload. Unfortunately, people who experience these symptoms or diseases tend to go to a conventional doctor, who prescribes medications to suppress the symptoms. The affected people do not end up feeling better and sometimes they feel worse because the medications add additional toxins to their bodies. Instead of getting rid of toxins, the medications add more toxins that eventually cause an additional toxic overload. Thus, it is highly recommended for you to detox or cleanse.

Anyone can benefit from detoxification. Detoxification or cleansing is important because it can literally reverse the symptoms of disease and improve your health significantly. It is a way to recharge, rejuvenate, renew, and jump-start your body for a more active and healthier life. The environment in a body with a toxic buildup is acidic. The detoxification process removes toxins and makes the environment in the body more alkaline. The more alkaline your body is, the healthier you are. Detoxing not only helps you lose weight, it also helps reboot your system, making

you feel alive, vibrant, full of energy, and, importantly, helps you to sleep better at night. Sleep deprivation is a huge complaint among people these days. Even just for improved sleep, detoxification is worth it.

There are many different types of detoxification protocols, and it is important to find one that works well for you. If you have not gone through a detox before, you may want to start gradually and use a gentle approach before you do a drastic and major juice cleanse. You do not have to do thirty-day juice cleanse to get the benefits of detoxification. Taking a yoga class, sitting in a sauna or a steam room, eating more fresh fruits and vegetables, or receiving acupuncture are a few examples of ways to gently detox your body. Juice cleanses are a wonderful way to cleanse your body. Drinking juice (juicing) rather than chewing or digesting food gives the digestive system a break so that it can renew and repair itself. Juicing floods the body with nutrients and antioxidants and helps strengthen the immune system. In addition, juicing has many more benefits, such as increasing energy, reducing blood pressure, repairing skin appearance, improving sleep, bettering memory, and aiding weight loss. Rather than doing a juice cleansing occasionally, many people incorporate juicing into their daily routine, and those individuals enjoy the myriad benefits that it has on their bodies. However, detoxing consists of not only juicing but also eating simple and natural foods of mostly vegetables and fruit without any sugar, flour, processed food, caffeine, alcohol, or tobacco.

Examples of side effects that accompany detoxification could be headache, nausea, fatigue, and trouble sleeping; however, these symptoms will disappear because they are only temporary, while you go through the detox process. When you decide to do a cleanse, keep in mind that it is wise to start slow and remember to consult with a trained health care professional before you begin.

During my three-week detoxification program at Hippocrates Health Institute, I attended daily lectures and workshops. In addition to drinking several green vegetable juice drinks per day, I ate a raw vegan diet that consisted mostly of raw vegetables, sprouts, nuts, and seeds. I also practiced yoga and qigong, exercised, and participated in various cutting-edge therapies as part of my detoxification process. All of these components together were needed to speed the healing process. I was rewarded with phenomenal results; I felt energetic, renewed, and finally healed. I highly recommend this amazing experience to everyone seeking alternate healing methods.

To this day, I still juice on a regular basis, at least a couple of times each week for health maintenance and disease prevention. I generally use vegetables, such as cucumber, spinach, and celery, and throw in some ginger root to spice it up. I also occasionally enjoy juice made of beets, carrots, and pineapple, and although this juice is higher in sugar, beets have many healing properties.

So to summarize, detoxification is used to remove toxins from the body, to reboot the body and bring it back to balance and full health. Think of detoxifying as a body tune-up, a super easy and quick way to supercharge your health. There are different types of detoxification programs available. Use the trial and error method to choose one that works best for you. That is, if a certain detoxification protocol does not work for you, try a different one. However, a method that does not work one time may work in the future because the effects depend on the level of toxins that you currently have. Although detoxing is a safe method to heal your body, it is recommended to do it, especially if you are very sick, under a doctor's supervision, so he or she can lead you through the process. Juicing is the most popular method of detoxification. It is safer to start gradually and use a mild method rather than an extensive and drastic one, allowing your body to ease into it so there are less side effects. Juicing has many benefits because it does not include fiber and therefore nutrients get absorbed on a cellular level. The digestive system is virtually bypassed and therefore gets a rest so it can repair itself. Most importantly, juicing removes toxins from body.

For more information about any of the topics mentioned in this chapter, please refer to the resources section under "Detox/ Cleansing."

- Most diseases are due to toxic buildup in the body.
- Detox is an excellent way to jump start your body.
- Juicing gives the digestive system a break so it can renew and repair itself.

Taly Cotler,
The Stressed Vegan

"Adopting the right attitude can convert
a negative stress into a positive one."

– Hans Selye

CHAPTER 6

Stress

Stress in a medical sense is a physical, mental, or emotional factor that causes bodily or mental tension. Stress can be external (from the environment or social situations) or internal (from a medical procedure or an illness). Stress is your body's way of responding to any kind of demand or threat. When you feel threatened, your nervous system responds by releasing a flood of the stress hormones adrenaline and cortisol to get your body ready for an emergency action. Your heart beats faster, blood pressure rises, muscles tighten, breath accelerates, and senses become sharper. These physical changes increase your strength and stamina, speed your reaction time, and enhance your focus. This is known as the "fight or flight" response, a complex reaction of the nervous and endocrine systems, and it is your body's way of protecting you.[45]

Stress within your comfort zone can help you perform under pressure, stay focused, energetic, and alert. It can also keep you safe when danger appears and motivate you to do your best. In emergency situations, stress can save your life—giving you extra strength to defend yourself, for example, spurring you to slam on the brakes to avoid a car accident. However, when stress becomes overwhelming, and it is beyond your comfort zone, it stops being helpful and causes devastating effects. Excessive stress is extremely detrimental to our bodies as well as to our minds, moods, and relationships, in the very least.

Unfortunately, modern life is full of deadlines and demands from both careers and family, causing much frustration and anxiety. In this busy, ever changing world, it is almost impossible to avoid daily stress. All of us experience stress through living our daily lives while carrying out our responsibilities and family obligations or from having things not turn out the way we expect them to. A simple example of being stressed is running late for work while you are caught in a traffic jam. This is an opportunity to become anxious and upset because you fear the inevitable late arrival to work. Stress is also caused by major life changes, such as getting married or divorced, the death of a loved one, moving to a new home, loss of a job, or financial troubles.

In addition to stress from overwhelming responsibilities, such as your family, job, or other obligations, self-imposed stress plays an important role. People experience self-imposed stress from different beliefs, fears, notions, and unreasonably high expectations of themselves. When you set up impossible and unrealistic goals for yourself, you set yourself up for a lot of negative emotions, including frustration and anxiety. A lot of disappointment is generated when you do not reach those goals or when things do not turn out the way you expected. This in itself can add additional unnecessary stress to your life and will affect your health. Another major source of stress is dealing with toxic people, those who create unnecessary drama on a regular basis in business or social environments. They can drain your energy and cause you to be overstressed. Therefore, it is crucial to learn how to set boundaries and protect yourself.

I have blood type A, and according to Dr. D'Adamo, people with this blood type tend to release more cortisol in reaction to stressful situations. Thus, with my blood type A, extremely stressful profession in IT, type A personality (leading to self-imposed stress even over small things, such as always being on time), raising two children mostly by myself, and very busy life, the stress was overwhelming. Despite my eating a healthy diet and staying fit, the cards were stacked against me. I have no doubt that excessive stress was a core factor in my illness.

Through the process of healing, I learned that if I did not manage my stress, I could never reach optimal health. Although adjusting my diet was fairly easy for me, slowing down was difficult. But being bedridden for a long time forced me to stop, think, and reflect on my life. I eventually concluded that I needed to manage stress better and to shift my stress response. I realized that my expectations of myself did not have to be so high; not everything in life has to be done thoroughly and perfectly. I decided not to sweat the small stuff and to cut myself some slack. I also examined my expectations of other people in social and business situations and decided to distance myself from drama and negativity. Not everyone thinks or acts like me, and everyone is different. I understand that most of us want everything to be predictable and precise, but that is not how life works out. Life sometimes is not fair and our paths have twists and turns. When things do not turn out the way we expect, we can get frustrated, angry or sad. I decided to change my response when things do not go the way I expect. Now I try to go with the flow and let life unfold. I realized that there is divine order, and sometimes we do not necessarily get what we want but instead we get what we need. So in addition to shifting my mindset, I decided to learn from adversity and grow spiritually. I channeled my energy in the right places and created new rules that supported my health. The specific techniques that I used are described in chapter 7.

The body's nervous system often does a poor job of distinguishing between daily stressors and life-threatening events. If you are stressed over an argument with a friend, a traffic jam on your commute, or a mountain of bills, for example, your body can still react as though you are facing a life-or-death situation. Not only that, many of us do not even realize how stressed we are. For most of us, stress is challenging, and we are not sure how to deal with it. By recognizing the symptoms and causes of stress, you can begin to reduce the detrimental effects it has on your body and mind as well as improve the quality of your life.

The signs and symptoms of chronic stress or stress overload depend on the level of stress you experience and your overall health. Keep in mind that not all people have all the symptoms and that they vary from one person to another. The following lists provide some of the common warning physical, cognitive, emotional, and behavioral signs and symptoms of chronic stress. The more signs and symptoms you notice in yourself, the closer you may be to stress overload. Physical symptoms may include aches and pains, nausea, dizziness, chest pain, rapid heart rate, digestive issues, impaired immune system, frequent colds or flu, and sleep disturbance. Cognitive symptoms may include memory problems, inability to concentrate, poor judgement, seeing only the negative, anxiety, racing thoughts, and constant worrying. Emotional symptoms may include depression, moodiness, irritability, anger, feeling overwhelmed, loneliness, isolation, or other mental or emotional health problems.

Behavioral symptoms may include increase or decrease in appetite, sleeping too much or too little, withdrawing from others, procrastinating or neglecting responsibilities, using alcohol or drugs to relax, and nervous habits (such as nail biting or pacing).[46]

Many people, but especially mothers, tend to spread themselves too thin by taking care of their family first without taking time off to take care of themselves. In general, we all tend to be very busy, running around trying to meet deadlines as well as dealing with the various obligations around us, and never stop to take a break. Therefore, we never give our bodies a chance to recoup after a stressful day, week, month, or even years. It is very simple: the body needs to LIVE, REST, and REPAIR! There is no doubt that we can handle stress better when we follow this rule. However, when stress is overwhelming, it becomes too much for our bodies to handle, and as a result, it has a significant detrimental effect on our health. A simple way to think of this rule is that it's like a bank account. You withdraw money (or energy) as you live, so you need to make a deposit (or rest and repair) to compensate for the withdrawal. If you never make a deposit (rest and repair), the balance in the bank account becomes less than zero. Your account is overdrawn (or stressed out). So consider finding a bit of time for yourself to do whatever it is that relaxes you. For example, some women find that they can make a deposit into their health account by meeting or calling a friend to chat or by treating themselves to a massage, pedicure, or facial.

Adrenal fatigue and its phases

Chronic stress is the malaise of the twenty-first century! Many people these days are overstressed and have adrenal fatigue but do not even realize it. Adrenal fatigue is a syndrome in which the adrenal glands stop producing a stress hormone called cortisol or secrete it at very low levels. This happens as a result of experiencing excess or chronic stress on a regular basis for an extended time.

Adrenal fatigue is a debilitating condition. A person with adrenal fatigue easily tires and cannot fully function or carry out daily responsibilities. The adrenal glands control many critical hormones in our bodies. All body parts are affected when the adrenal glands are not performing optimally. Illnesses associated with adrenal fatigue include chronic fatigue syndrome, fibromyalgia, ovarian-adrenal-thyroid imbalance syndrome, estrogen dominance, and hypothy-roidism. However, it is not considered a medical diagnosis nor is it well known by conventional (Western) medicine practitioners.

The adrenal glands are an endocrine gland located above each kidney that produces hormones, including adrenaline and cortisol. There are various stages of adrenal fatigue, when the adrenal glands function below or above the necessary level, with symptoms increas-ing in severity at each stage. It starts as adrenal fatigue (known as being hypo adrenal) and can lead to adrenal exhaustion or burnout. Early stages of adrenal fatigue are characterized by low production of cortisol, lack of energy, and extreme fatigue that is not improved by a good night's sleep. Although you may still get a good night's sleep at this stage, you do not feel refreshed in the morning. On the other end of the scale, adrenal exhaustion (known as being hyper adrenal) is associated with the excessive production of cortisol, and although you are extremely exhausted, you sleep very little for weeks and sometimes months. Regardless of the stage, many people with adrenal fatigue also have fibromyalgia.[47]

The most severe stage leads to serious adrenal diseases, includ-ing Addison's disease or Cushing's syndrome. Addison's disease is characterized by a total deficiency or an insufficient production of cortisol. By contrast, Cushing's Syndrome is caused by excessive production of cortisol. In very advanced stages of adrenal fatigue, a person may develop postural tachycardia syndrome (POTS), which I developed due to excessive production of cortisol.

Adrenal dysfunction and its various stages have been recognized as distinct clinical syndromes since the turn of the twentieth century. However, most conventionally trained physicians are still unfamiliar with this condition because it is difficult to diagnose through tradi-tional blood tests. Most patients are sent home with antidepressants after a short trial of hormonal replacement therapy or a steroid regimen, but these treatments usually fail.

Although we cannot totally eliminate stress from our lives, we can change the way we react to stressful situations or events. It is crucial to manage stress and keep it under control before it controls us. Stress can be very helpful, but when it is out of control, it can have a significant negative effect on our health. I know it can be challenging, but we must stop in the midst of our busy lives and take a break to relieve our stress. In addition to eating a healthy diet, there is a wide spectrum of stress management techniques that can be used to control the level of stress a person experiences, including relaxing, take a few deep breaths, meditating, engaging in a physical activity like yoga, and getting a good night's sleep. Please refer to chapter 7 for a deeper explanation and more details on relaxation techniques.

Sleep is critical to all aspects of our lives and is very important for our bodies. During sleep, our bodies repair and rejuvenate, and our cells are renewed and regenerated. As I previously mentioned, when we live and exert ourselves for long periods without any rest or sleep, our bodies do not have a chance to repair, and therefore we get sick. Sleep deprivation can make us more sensitive to stressful events, which can lead us to experience even more stress. The quality and the amount of sleep we get can influence how we react emotionally to stressful events.

It is recommended to sleep at least eight hours every night. If possible, sleep should be from a set specific time until another set specific time. It is not recommended to sleep right after a meal because the food can cause digestive issues as well as interrupt our sleep. It is also important to eat a light meal and to avoid coffee, alcohol, or mind-stimulating activities, such as watching TV, especially the news, using a computer, or listening to loud music, at night. Create a calming ritual for yourself before bedtime. You can try meditating or listening to relaxing music.

For those of us who have sleep problems, either having a difficult time falling asleep or falling asleep but waking up in the in middle of the night, it may be an indication that our hormones, such as cortisol, progesterone, or estrogen, are out of balance. Another reason for experiencing sleep issues especially as we age is a lack of melatonin in our bodies. Melatonin production, which is important for sleep, declines as we age.

There are many negative effects of chronic stress. It is believed that chronic stress, rather than an unhealthy diet, is the number one cause of disease. I have seen many people whose diets were unhealthy but who had no stress or reacted to stress in a much healthier way and were not sick. By contrast, I have seen people who ate healthy diets but experienced chronic stress and were sick. The bodies of people who suffer from various illnesses as well as from excessive stress do not heal rapidly. The healing process is influenced by stress, and regardless of what disease a person may have, if cortisol levels are out of the normal range, it will take that person longer to heal.

Stress is a key factor in health and is dangerous when not properly managed. In my opinion, a course about stress should be taught in schools as part of the core curriculum, but reality is different. In our society, students are encouraged to take many rigorous classes. They become stressed at a young age. Then they graduate and work in corporate America, where overworking is expected. Thus, many people, young and old are so overwhelmed with too many activities, demands, and obligations that our future generations may experience adrenal fatigue at younger ages.

In addition to eating a healthy diet and using relaxation techniques, such as meditation and yoga, certain vitamin supplements and herbs may be taken to overcome adrenal fatigue and bring the adrenal glands back into balance. A protocol that may help one person may not help another, and therefore treatment is based on trial and error. If you suspect that you have chronic stress issues, you may want to check with a health care professional. However, rather than seeking a conventional medicine practitioner, I recommend visiting a holistic or integrative medicine practitioner and asking them to run diagnostic tests that measure your cortisol levels.

Be aware that cortisol levels fluctuate throughout the day. Because a blood test can check the cortisol level only at the specific time of day that the blood was drawn, such a test is not a good option. A health care practitioner familiar with adrenal fatigue would instead order either a saliva or urine test, either of which provides more comprehensive results and is therefore more accurate than the blood test. Make sure to use stress management techniques to get stress under control before it controls you.

For more information about any of the topics mentioned in this chapter, please refer to the resources section under "Stress."

- Keep your stress under control before it controls you.
- Our body needs to Live, Rest, and Repair!

Taly Cotler,
The Stressed Vegan

"If you change the way you look at things,
the things you look at change."

— Wayne Dyer

CHAPTER 7

Healing the Mind

In our hectic lives, we need to be able to stop in the midst of busyness, tune out the noise of life and just be still. You will get an emotional relief as well as physical and spiritual one. The result can be a greater inner peace, understanding, and clarity. Healing and transforming my mind was much more challenging than healing my body. During my journey of healing, I was forced to slow down, reflect, and practice mind control. With the help of the healing methods described in this chapter, I was able to control my thoughts and change my mindset. I specifically used deep breathing, mindfulness, guided imagery and the Silva method.

Deep breathing was very challenging for me at times because my heart rate was elevated. But the more I practiced deep and slow breaths, the easier it got. Now I practice deep breaths not only at stressful times but also throughout the day. Deep breathing is a powerful way to lower the heart rate and cortisol levels, and it is a path to relaxation. When you are presented with a stressful situation, stop and take a few deep and slow breaths instead of reacting. After some practice, you will notice it becomes a habit and it will help you to deal with stress better.

Practicing mindfulness means to focus on the now rather than the past or future. I tried my best to focus on my healing rather than thinking about the past and the sequence of events that led to my illness. I had been frustrated that despite my healthy lifestyle I had become very ill. I also harbored anger and frustration over the many misdiagnoses of my illness by conventional Western doctors. However, during my reflections, I realized that although they were unable to diagnose or treat me, each one provided a bit of information that helped me to cope or led me to the decisions that I made along the way. Their lack of knowledge about my condition, forced me to search for alternative methods to heal myself.

Guided imagery helped me to imagine myself strong, energetic, healed and to dissolve all negative emotions that I had regarding my experience. It also helped me to better cope with stress. The Silva method is a powerful tool that teaches specialized guided imagery techniques and it helped me to develop mind control. I was able to literally reprogram my mind to select positive thoughts and to ignore negative ones. I realized that the way my mind was wired and my thinking patterns actually brought on my adrenal fatigue. I regularly practiced mind healing techniques, and this practice helped me be in charge of my healing process. It required a lot of practice, but it was truly an amazing process and experience.

All the tools that I acquired cultivated my new state of mind and helped me to develop new healthier habits and self-awareness. Once I saw such positive results in all areas, I began to have faith that my illness would be reversed. I still use these tools to deal with life. I believe there is a reason for everything and that most situations can be turned around and that this change is all for the better.

What follows are some mind-healing tools for you to explore that might help keep your stress level under control. A lot of research has gone into understanding how mind healing works. It is clear that your mind can and does heal your body. What appears to be understood is that the healing powers of the mind lie in the subconscious. The subconscious aims to create agreement between what it believes and reality. It accepts what you believe as truth and reacts according to those beliefs.[48] Heal your mind and your body will follow. But how do you heal your mind? There are a few techniques to heal the mind. Meditation is one of them.

What is meditation?

The word meditation carries different meanings in different contexts. Meditation has been practiced for many years as a component of numerous religious traditions and beliefs. It often involves an internal effort to self-regulate, train, or transform the mind in some way. The term meditation refers to a broad variety of practices that includes techniques designed to promote relaxation, build internal energy or life force (also known as qi or prana), and develop compassion, love, patience, generosity, and forgiveness. Meditation is a powerful tool and is often used to clear the mind and ease many health concerns. There are many things in life that are beyond our control. However, it is possible to take responsibility for our own states of mind and to change them for the better. According to Buddhism, meditating is the most important thing we can do. Buddhism teaches that meditating is the only real antidote to personal sorrows, anxieties, fears, hatreds, and general confusion that beset the human condition.[49]

Buddhist meditation practices are techniques that encourage and develop concentration, clarity, emotional positivity, and a calm

seeing of the true nature of things. By engaging with a particular meditation practice, you learn the patterns and habits of your mind, and the practice offers a means to cultivate new, more positive ways of being. With regular work and patience, these nourishing, focused states of mind can deepen into profoundly peaceful and energized states of mind. Such experiences can have a transformative effect and can lead to a new understanding of life.

In my opinion, meditation is the process of quieting and emptying the mind, and when the mind wanders, bringing it back. Regardless of what type of meditation practice is chosen, the more deep and slow breaths that are taken, the more the body heals. Meditation heals both the body and the mind, so the healing power is actually within your control. During meditation, all thoughts and worries are removed from your mind by narrowing your focus, shutting out the external world, and keeping your body still.

Benefits of meditation

Studies have shown that there are both physical and mental health benefits to meditation. Nothing has more power to heal and transform the body than the mind. Stress reduction could be the key to meditation's beneficial effect on health. According to research, meditation not only lowers stress hormone levels but also lowers blood pressure, strengthens the immune system, and improves mood and sleep.[50]

In addition, meditation improves the ability to concentrate and increase your conscious awareness. With a regular practice of meditation, your body undergoes a change, with every cell filled with more energy, which results in joy, peace, and enthusiasm. Meditation also brings the brain wave pattern into a relaxed state that promotes physical and mental healing. As a result, anxiety decreases while happiness increases, the mind is sharpened, and the focus is increased. Meditation can also balance both the right and left hemispheres of the brain, enabling them to work in harmony.[51]

According to research, people who meditate daily, even for as little as twenty minutes, have lower cortisol levels and are able to reduce stress in their lives. Life can be very stressful, with our daily challenges, meeting deadlines, carrying the responsibility of having a family, and making sure that all their needs are met. Many of us do more than we should. Our minds are overstimulated with outside noise and distractions of news, social media, and email, and we tend to exert ourselves to a point of exhaustion. Not only do our bodies need a break, but most importantly, our minds need a break. This is when meditation plays an important role; by giving the mind a break, we can actually reset both our minds and bodies.

There is no doubt that meditation improves both physical and emotional responses to stress. Western science has not yet connected the dots between what happens in the meditating brain and the immune system. But one University of Wisconsin study found increased electrical activity in regions of the left frontal lobe, an area that tends to be more active in optimistic people, after eight weeks of training in meditation. According to other research, meditation activates the parts of the brain that stop performing while under stress.[52]

Types of meditation and relaxation techniques

There are dozens of specific styles of meditation practice. Those that I prefer and that are mostly practiced include deep breathing, mindfulness, Transcendental Meditation (TM), progressive muscle relaxation, and guided imagery/visualization. Hypnotherapy and the Silva method are techniques that are very helpful to train and reprogram the mind.

Regardless of the technique practiced, meditation has a significant and positive effect on the body and is very beneficial to health. Even if you are skeptical, why not give it a try and see the results? I promise that once you notice the benefits, you will become addicted to meditation. Next I describe of each type of meditation that I mentioned.

Deep breathing

"Deep Breathing is one of the most effective ways to start meditating and can be performed anywhere. The two key elements of any meditation practice are finding a focal point and letting go of any thoughts or emotions that arise. Focusing on your deep, rhythmic breath helps turn your mind inward and activates your parasympathetic nervous system, which promotes relaxation."[53]

Deep breathing helps you to stop thinking, control your racing thoughts, and rest your mind. Deep breathing is free and available to us anytime, anywhere, yet it is powerful and beneficial. Take a deep, slow breath, filling your lungs with fresh air. Take fewer and slower breaths, rather than fast and shallow breaths. These slow, deep breaths actually help us calm ourselves and bring our stress levels and stress responses under control. By taking deep breaths, we expand our lung volume and increase our lung capacity. So merely by modifying our breathing, we can reduce stress. Blood pressure is governed by our sympathetic nervous system. The sympathetic nervous system is a messenger of the stress response. Both breathing and regulating your thoughts have a positive impact on the sympathetic nervous system.

Deep breathing is so easy that it may be done while sitting, standing, walking, or lying down. You may want to close your eyes while practicing this type of meditation to help close out all outside noise and stimuli to make this practice more powerful and beneficial. Obviously closing your eyes should not be done while walking or driving. I like to repeatedly take a slow, deep breath while thinking: *I inhale positive and healing energy that heals each and every cell of my body*, and then slowly exhale while thinking *I exhale all negativity, stress, and tension*. Start with five to ten deep breaths, increasing the number over time. The more you practice deep breathing, the faster you heal and restore your health.[54]

Progressive muscle relaxation

This technique teaches you how to relax your muscles through a two-step process. First, you systematically tense particular muscle groups in your body, such as your neck and shoulders. Next, you release the tension and notice how your muscles feel when you relax them. You start with the top of your body and then go down to each part or organ of your body until you reach the bottom. From head to toe, you name each part one at a time in your mind, tense it, and then release it. At the end of the practice, you will feel wonderfully relaxed.

Mindfulness

Another of my favorite meditation practices is mindfulness, which also comes from the Buddhist tradition. The Buddhist term "sati" translates to "mindfulness" and breathes life into the practice. Mindfulness is the psychological process of bringing one's attention to the internal and external experiences occurring in the present moment, which can be developed through the practice of meditation and other training.

Mindfulness is all about acknowledging emotions, sensations, and thoughts by letting the mind wander, accepting any thoughts that come up (rather than resisting them), and then letting them go. Mindfulness is focusing on your breathing, and understanding the now or the present moment without drifting into concerns about the past or future. It is fairly easy: merely close your eyes, take a deep breath, tune in, and listen to all the thoughts that come up. You focus on your breath, block out any outside noise, and calm your mind to receive information and answers that are within each of us. You can try breathing in and out through your nose with your focus on the third eye, located on the forehead between the eyebrows, which represents our intuition or the sixth chakra.

Mindfulness uses all of our five senses: sight, smell, hearing, taste, and touch. During a mindfulness meditation session, we can, for example, imagine that we are enjoying beautiful flowers, seeing, smelling, and touching them. We can also imagine that we hear birds chirping or the sound of water flowing in a nearby river or ocean or that we taste something sweet, such as chocolate.

Research has indicated that the practice of mindfulness is strongly correlated with greater well-being and perceived health. Mindfulness meditation may ease anxiety and mental stress. Although meditation is not yet mainstream, mindfulness meditation has become more popular in recent years. Studies done by researchers at Johns Hopkins University in Baltimore, Maryland, have shown that mindfulness-based interventions are effective in the reduction of stress, anxiety, depression, and pain.[55]

Transcendental Meditation

Transcendental Meditation (TM) refers to a specific form of mantra meditation called the Transcendental Meditation technique. Maharishi Mahesh Yogi, who was a spiritual guru, introduced the TM technique and TM movement in India in the mid-1950s. It is now one of the most widely practiced and researched meditation techniques. The TM technique involves closing your eyes and repeating a sound or a mantra for fifteen to twenty minutes twice daily. According to the TM movement, it is a method for relaxation, stress reduction, and self-development.[56]

In this Hindu tradition, you sit in lotus pose, internally chant a mantra, and focus on rising above the negativity. People who practice this method of meditation experience an inner calmness and serenity even when they are dynamically busy. The mantra is chosen by a teacher (guru) based on its suitability to the individual meditator. Meditation has a calming effect and directs awareness inward, that is, being awake inside without being aware of anything outside.

The sound of the mantra is the object of your attention. You can chant the sound out loud or internally. When you chant the mantra internally, the "inner sound" becomes the object of attention for your meditation. When you chant the mantra out loud, the sound of the mantra becomes the focus. However, you may also focus on the effects of the sound vibrations in your body, in your breathing, and in the feeling of the mantra on your mouth, lips, and tongue.

Some people prefer chanting a mantra rather than focusing on their breathing while meditating. Although in both cases we can control our thoughts, some people find it easier to control their thoughts while chanting a mantra rather than focusing on breathing, especially when the mantra is chanted aloud. During a TM session, the mantra being chanted overwrites our thoughts.

The most common mantras are om shanti shanti, peace, God, or a combination of syllables. The mantra can be repeated as many times as you wish and for as long as desired. Regardless of whether the mantra is being chanted out loud or silently, everyone who chants experiences overall calmness and peace.[57]

Guided imagery/visualization

Imagery or visualization involves using your imagination to help your body relax. Your body can become stressed and tense in response to thoughts that make you anxious or upset. Your body can also become more calm and relaxed in response to pleasant and cheerful thoughts.

One way you can use imagery or visualization is to close your eyes and imagine being in a place that is peaceful. You can use mental images as well as your five senses of sight, hearing, taste, touch, and smell. Imagery can also include texture and temperature. For example, you can imagine a quiet beach, a fireplace, or a field of flowers. You hear and see the waves, the logs crackling on the fire, or birds circling and calling; you smell the salty air, the burning wood, or the flowers; you feel the sand, the heat, or the wind on your skin.

Using our five senses is what guided imagery/visualization has in common with mindfulness meditation. I used it to imagine myself completely healed. What an amazing experience!

This technique can be practiced on your own or guided by a trained practitioner, who would help you to generate mental images. The practitioner may facilitate this process in person to an individual or a group. Alternatively, you may follow guidance provided by an aural recording, video, or audio visual media comprising spoken instruction, any of which may be accompanied by music or sound.[58] For beginners, this is a great option because they are guided through each step of the meditation. Once beginners practice this meditation style for a while, they may no longer need guidance and can practice on their own.

Hypnotherapy

Meditation and hypnotherapy use very similar entry techniques to relax and calm the mind and are both very powerful self-development tools. However, hypnotherapy focuses on the subconscious and delves into very deep concentrative states that help to reprogram bad habits and negative thought patterns.

It is a powerful tool that helps achieve effective changes in your life on all levels, physical, emotional, and mental. Hypnosis is the induction of a state of consciousness in which a person apparently loses the power of voluntary action and is highly responsive to suggestion or direction. It is a tool that helps with many health issues as well as an auto immune disorder. Hypnosis has been used as a supplemental approach to cognitive behavioral therapy since 1949.

Licensed physicians and psychologists may use hypnosis to treat depression and to alleviate stress and anxiety. Hypnosis is also used to treat eating or sleeping disorders, post traumatic stress, and even gambling disorder. Certified hypnotherapists, who are not physicians or psychologists, often use hypnosis to help patients overcome fears and phobias, control bad habits, such as smoking, and promote weight loss. Modern hypnotherapy has reported great success in treating these issues.[59]

Silva method

The Silva method, previously known as Silva Mind Control, is a self-help program developed by José Silva. The Silva method teaches students guided imagery techniques intended to "rewire" their subconscious and negative programming. It taps into a person's true potentials to achieve their goals using a meditation technique and mental training program that is offered in seminars internationally.

It is a powerful tool that claims to increase an individual's abilities through relaxation and development of higher brain functions. Proponents believe that it can improve a person's self-image, sense of personal well-being, clarity of thought, and ability to overcome conditions, such as nicotine addiction. Silva believed that it could be used to develop paranormal abilities, such as intuition and extra sensory perception (ESP, or what is also known as the sixth sense), and that it could tap into higher consciousness. The technique aims to reach and sustain a state of mental functioning, called the alpha state, in which brain wave frequency is seven to fourteen hertz. Daydreaming and the transition to sleeping are alpha states.

The Silva method helps develop memory, concentration, relaxation, creativity, intuition, positive thinking, and more. It helps overcome stress and fears as well as improves many health issues, such as fatigue, insomnia, headaches, and overeating. It is a powerful tool that helped me to alleviate stress and to heal. It helps us learn how to control our thoughts and change or overwrite the negative thoughts to positive ones. It helps transform certain thought and behavior patterns to help you see things in a perspective that will be more beneficial to your well-being. Once you start practicing this method, you will notice many health benefits that will help heal both your mind and body.[60]

Meditation summary

To effectively learn how to practice meditation, I recommend taking classes, if desired, but there are also internet resources and apps that may be used. My suggestion is to try all types of meditation that you come across, and see which one helps you achieve that level of inner peace you are seeking. Once you have found your favorite meditation method, incorporate it into your daily schedule to best combat the enormous levels of stress in your life. You can even incorporate and alternate several types of meditation practice into your daily routine. However, to experience the benefits of meditation, you must practice regularly. It takes only a few minutes every day. Once embedded in the daily routine, meditation will soon become the best part of your day as you very quickly notice its positive results on your well-being.

For more information about any of the topics mentioned in this chapter, please refer to the resources section under "Healing the Mind."

- Daily meditation is beneficial to your health.
- Take deep breaths throughout the day.
- Heal your mind and your body will follow.

Taly Cotler,
The Stressed Vegan

"To enjoy the glow of good health,
you must exercise."

– Gene Tunney

Chapter 8

Physical Activity

When I was younger I worked out intensively: I did cardiovascular training, lifted weights, played basketball, swam, danced, and practiced yang yoga, which is a relatively intense form. As I became older, I lowered the intensity of my physical activity. Now I exercise moderately, that is, I still lift weights and do cardio workouts and yang yoga, but they are less intense than when I was younger, and I have also incorporated the less intense yin yoga into my exercise routine. I started practicing yoga more than 25 years ago, and I have tried all the styles that are mentioned in this chapter. I have taken yoga classes in studios, fitness centers, or retreats in different places around the world. I practice yoga daily to help me stay centered and relaxed. When I go on vacation and miss a few days of yoga, I literally feel out of balance.

When it comes to exercise, we each determine what we can or cannot do and how hard we want to push ourselves. Some people follow the all-or-nothing principle, believing that if exercise is going to be good for you, it has to be hard and even painful. This is an absolute myth and very far from the truth. In the 1990s, a shift occurred in exercise recommendations as experts began to recognize the benefits of "moderate intensity" activity. So before you go out and injure yourself trying to get in some hardcore exercise, step back and take a moment to develop a workout routine that you might actually stick with and enjoy. After all, the more you enjoy an experience, the more likely you are to repeat it.

Regular physical activity is one of the most important things you can do for your health. Physical activity on a regular basis helps improve your overall health and fitness and reduces your risk of many chronic diseases. For example, regular physical activity can help control your weight, and reduce your risk of cardiovascular disease, diabetes, and cancer. Among other benefits, it strengthens your bones and muscles and improves your mental health and mood by releasing chemicals called endorphins. These endorphins trigger a positive feeling in the body described as euphoric. That feeling, also called a runner's high, can be accompanied by a positive and energizing outlook on life. Physical activity also improves your ability to perform daily activities. It definitely increases your chances of living longer. Exercise not only makes you feel good but also has long-term benefits and prevents falls, especially if you are an older adult.[61]

Many types of physical activity are considered cardio, including running, swimming, walking, bicycling, dancing. There is also weight-lifting, yoga, qigong, and many others too numerous to list here. In Dr. D'Adamo's book *Eat Right 4 Your Type*, he recommends exercising based on your blood type. For instance, he suggests yoga or tai chi for people with blood type A and vigorous aerobic exercises, with caution and within your limits, such as jogging, biking, and weight lifting, for those with blood type O. Lower impact cardio workouts, such as tennis and cycling, are recommended for people with blood type B, and more gentle exercise, such as walking, hiking, golf, yoga, or dance for those with blood type AB.

Personal trainers recommend engaging in thirty minutes or more of physical activity at least three to four times every week. You can do thirty consecutive minutes or break it into ten-minute segments throughout the day. Thirty minutes a day is enough to maintain health and reduce your risk of chronic disease. If you want to lose weight or gain additional benefits and further improve your health, you will need to exercise for a longer duration and at a higher intensity. Brisk walking is the most popular choice of physical activity because it can easily be incorporated into a busy day, has low injury rates, doesn't require special skills or equipment, and can be performed by almost everyone at any age.

Numerous studies have shown that moderate exercise is good, whereas excessive exercise is damaging. I believe that a good rule of thumb to follow in life is that everything should be done in moderation, and that includes physical activity. When exercise is performed in moderation, there is less risk of injury. Moderation and variety are the keys. When you plan an exercise program, include a variety of exercises to ensure that you work out different muscles each time, which also helps prevent injury. A variety of workouts makes it more fun, challenging, and less boring. Choose whatever physical activities that you enjoy most and that can easily become part of your routine.

Regardless of whether you work out by yourself or with a personal trainer, exercise with caution. Sometimes trainers tend to push their clients too hard, requiring rigorous exercise that may lead to unnecessary injuries. Therefore it is crucial to listen to your body to prevent injuries. Also, the amount, duration, intensity or frequency of your exercise should be based on your goals and time availability. Begin slowly, giving your body time to adjust and working up to the desired amount and intensity. If you have any or at risk of any chronic health problems (e.g., heart disease, diabetes, or obesity), consult your physician before starting any physical activity.

Weight training

Weight training should be included in your workout plan because of its many benefits, especially for people who are more than 40 years old and are experiencing bone loss.

Not only does strength training increase your physical work capacity, it also improves your ability to perform activities of daily living. You will be able to work harder and longer with the incorporation of proper weight training activities. It improves bone density—weight training is one of the best ways you can control bone loss as you age. It increases the strength of the connective tissue, muscles and tendons, and this leads to improved motor performance and decreased injury risk. It improves your quality of life and helps you gain body confidence. Strength training not only makes you strong, builds muscles, and increases flexibility and overall fitness, it also helps manage your weight. Using free weights is considered safer than using weight machines.

<u>Yoga</u>

Many people have misconceptions about yoga practice. They think it is either too slow or too complicated. They have the notion that yoga requires a high level of flexibility to perform advanced poses. On the contrary, yoga caters to every age and every level of flexibility. Everyone who practices yoga can adjust it to their own pace and difficulty level. There is no competition! Even for the elderly or physically challenged, there is chair yoga that has enormous benefits. The many benefits of yoga include enhanced mind-body connection, mindfulness, mind control, focus, and physical flexibility as well as decrease in stress.

Yoga is a Hindu physical, spiritual, and mental practice or discipline that is widely practiced for health and relaxation. It includes breath control, simple meditation, and the adoption of specific body postures. Yoga means "union" because it integrates the mind, body, and spirit. Yoga is not only a physical, emotional, and spiritual practice, it is also a union with the "self," which helps you to be more in tune with your body and to develop self-awareness. In addition, yoga changes the activities of neurons in the brain and affects neurotransmitters, as has been shown in several scientific studies.[62]

I have practiced many different yoga styles throughout my life as it became a bigger part of my routine. I practice yoga daily, either on my own or by taking a class at a studio. When I practice on my own, I do not practice a specific style but make my own routine, and it is different each day. Most any exercise performed regularly is great, but I strongly believe that yoga is much more powerful and has many more health benefits than many other types of exercise. However, incorporating both yoga and other types of exercise into your workout regimen would be ideal.

Benefits

The physical benefits of yoga include increased flexibility, muscle strength and tone, and improved respiration, energy, and vitality. I have noticed over the many years that I have practiced yoga that it has increased my flexibility and strength and has helped me to better control my breathing and thereby stay balanced, relaxed, and centered. More benefits of yoga are that it helps maintain balanced metabolism, weight reduction, cardio and circulatory health, improved athletic performance, and protection from injury. Yoga can create transformations in your body and mind. It offers mental benefits and has the power to change your brain. Scientific studies have shown that yoga practice can have a positive effect on the neurotransmitters in the brain. Yoga offers numerous poses and breathing techniques. Your breath can calm your nervous system and in turn help relieve stress. On an energy level, yoga removes energy blockages and balances the body's energy centers, called chakras, which helps restore health.[63]

By stretching your body into different directions, yoga poses create space in the body, which helps with healing. A few yoga poses include twists and holding poses that temporarily constrict the blood flow into that area. Once the pose is released, the blood flow returns, bringing a fresh, healing supply of oxygen to that area. Taking deep breaths during a yoga practice also supplies our cells with a fresh supply of oxygen.

A few common yoga poses include child's pose, tree, downward-facing dog, upward-facing dog, warrior, chair, and triangle. At the end of a yoga practice, we say "namaste," a gesture that represents the belief that there is a divine spark within each of us that is located in the heart chakra. The gesture is an acknowledgement of the soul in one person by the soul in another.

Yoga styles

There are many yoga styles, but next I will cover the most common ones and those that I have practiced. There are two main yoga categories, yang and yin. The former is more dynamic and the latter is a slower, more meditative style. I consider hatha, vinyasa, and Bikram to be styles grouped under the yang category, whereas yin and restorative yoga I consider to be styles of the yin category. I will also cover Kundalini yoga which is an "energetic breath" style.

I will discuss the styles in the yang category first. As I said, yang yoga is a term used to describe the more dynamic and active forms of yoga. Yang yoga poses often emphasize strength and endurance. They are active and powerful and generate heat in the body.

Hatha

Hatha yoga is the most widely practiced form of yoga in the United States. It is the branch of yoga that focuses on physical health and mental well-being. Hatha yoga uses bodily postures (asanas), breathing techniques (pranayama), and meditation (dhyana). There are nearly 200 hatha yoga postures, with hundreds of variations, to promote circulation in all the organs, glands, and tissues. Hatha yoga poses also stretch and align the body, promoting balance and flexibility. Hatha yoga focuses on breathing, and its goal is to create a healthy body and a clear peaceful mind.[64]

Vinyasa

Vinyasa, also known as "power" or "flow" yoga, is a powerful, energetic form of yoga. During the practice, students fluidly move from one pose to the next while connecting their breathing to their movements. This type of yoga is sometimes taught in a heated studio, which makes it a vigorous and revitalizing form of physical fitness. It is an active and athletic style of yoga adapted from the traditional Ashtanga system of the late 1980s. Vinyasa type classes that last sixty to ninety minutes can be vastly different depending on teacher preference, but all are based on a fixed sequence of poses known as the Sun Salutation. It is a set of twelve yoga asanas that bring the body, breath, and mind together. It offers many health benefits, such as strength, flexibility, and balance.[65] Although it also offers many other benefits, such as balancing the chakras, I recommend it mostly to younger people who are looking for a fast paced cardio workout. Many adults practice it, but it may be a bit intense for older people.

Bikram

Bikram yoga is a system that Bikram Choudhury synthesized from traditional hatha yoga and popularized beginning in the early 1970s. It consists of a series of twenty-six challenging postures, with many being balancing poses, including standing bow, eagle, and tree poses.[66]

During the standing bow pose, you stand on one foot and lift the other foot and leg up in the air and stand still for ninety seconds. Balancing on one foot for that length of time requires that you stop thinking and focus on a focal point and nothing else. This pose helps balance the right and left hemispheres of the brain. For me, this pose was very challenging at first, and I almost tipped over a few times. However, with time it became one of my favorite poses. In general, this yoga style helps to relax your body and totally clear your mind.

Practicing the "Standing Bow Pose" at a Yoga retreat in Costa Rica.

Bikram yoga is a hot yoga style, ideally practiced in a room heated to a high temperature. The heat helps the body to be more flexible and stretch further than it could in colder temperatures. I practiced this type of yoga for seven years, and at first it was very challenging. However, after practicing for some time, I would emerge from a class with my mind completely clear. It was one of my favorite yoga styles when I used to practice the more dynamic yang yoga.

Next I discuss two yin category of yoga styles. Yin helped me to slow down when I was recovering my health. I would emerge from a class floating as though I had just received a massage, feeling the impact of yin yoga throughout my entire day. It reminded me to slow down and that was the key to my healing. There is much power in stillness.

Yin

Yin is a quiet, slow paced, and meditative yoga style, also called Taoist yoga. In a yin practice, poses are held for a longer time, ranging from one to five minutes. Yin focuses on lengthening connective tissues and is meant to complement yang yoga. Yin yoga poses apply moderate stress to the connective tissues of the body—the tendons, fascia, and ligaments—with the aim of increasing circulation in the joints and improving flexibility. Yin poses are passive, meaning you are supposed to relax your muscles and let gravity do the work. These poses develop patience. Yin yoga is an excellent practice for older people because there is only a slight chance of being injured.[67]

Restorative

Restorative yoga is the centering of your breath and body, aligning the physical and mental by practicing stillness or gentle movements for extended periods of time. You will spend as many as twenty minutes each in just four or five simple poses (often they are modifications of standard postures) using props like blankets, bolsters, and soothing lavender eye pillows to help you sink into deep relaxation. The props assist you in holding the poses longer. Restorative yoga is an excellent way to disconnect from the hectic activity of daily life and let your speedometer return to zero mph. This yoga style definitely requires less work, with more emphasis placed on relaxing and calming the entire body and mind.

Kundalini

Kundalini yoga, also known as laya, siddha, or sahaja yoga, is a widely performed spiritual practice. This practice features constantly moving, invigorating asanas (postures), pranayama (breathing), mantras, and meditation.

Different from the hatha yoga's pranayama practices, the breathing exercises associated with kundalini yoga are more centered on alternate nostril breathing. Alternate nostril breathing is known to increase lung capacity and restore balance in the right and left hemispheres of the brain.

This is a systemized form of spiritual practice aimed at releasing the kundalini energy in your body. The primary focus of yoga asanas is to cleanse the impurities at the physical and mental levels. The poses are systemized to empower the nervous and glandular systems, energizing them so that the flow of the life force (prana) is not interrupted.[68]

Yoga conclusion

I encourage you to try a yoga class either at a local studio or at a gym. Consider striking a balance between yang and yin yoga. Regardless of what style is practiced, yoga is beneficial to both your body and mind. The feeling after taking a yoga class is amazing. Yoga poses help lower the stress hormone cortisol and manages the stress response. If you do not like a particular style or a teacher, do not give up; try a different one. After practicing yoga for a while, you will notice and experience the tremendous transformative power that it offers. Yoga improves your energy level, strengthens your immune system, improves your sleep and mood, and alleviates back pain among other benefits. Yoga is so beneficial that if you merely practice a few poses a day, you will soon begin to notice a tremendous difference.

Qigong

Qigong is considered a healing art. It consists of coordinated body poses and flowing movement, deep breathing, and meditation that are mostly used for health and spirituality. With its roots in Chinese medicine, qigong is traditionally viewed as a practice to achieve balance of chi, or life energy. Qigong is practiced worldwide for relaxation and self-healing. As a form of gentle exercise, qigong is composed of movements that are typically repeated, stretching the body, increasing blood or lymph flow, and enhancing balance. It improves posture, balance, respiration, and the ability to relax. Qigong is a form of meditation that uses the breath to circulate energy through the body and energy centers. The focused combination of breathing, movement, and meditation helps individuals control their reactions to stress.

Qigong and tai chi are similar, and both are practiced to balance chi. Tai chi is mainly practiced today as an excellent form of exercise with many health benefits. This gentle form of exercise can help maintain strength, flexibility, balance, and also wellness. "Tai chi is often described as 'meditation in motion,' but it might well be called 'medication in motion.'" Harvard Medical School endorses both qigong and tai chi.[69]

Summary

Varying your workout is essential for improving physical fitness as well as for preventing boredom. I vary my workout routines and even the types of yoga I practice. Your body may require a vigorous workout one day and a more gentle practice on another day. Regardless of the type of physical activity you integrate into your daily routine, it will offer myriad benefits to your health. The amount, duration, intensity, and frequency of exercise that you need are based on your goals and available time. Learn to recognize the signs that your body gives you and know your limits. The key is everything in moderation. After all, you exercise to keep your body healthy, not to injure it. Before committing to any exercise routine, check with your doctor or a health care professional.

For more information about any of the topics discussed in this chapter, please refer to the resources section under "Physical Activity."

- Yoga offers endless benefits to your body and mind.
- Weight training increases bone density.
- Alternate your cardio exercise routine.
- Moderation and variety are the keys to exercise.

"Natural healing is about taking control of your life and being responsible for everything that goes in and out of your body, mind and spirit."

— Richard Schulze

Taly Cotler,
The Stressed Vegan

CHAPTER 9

Healing Modalities

This chapter compares holistic and conventional medicine approaches, providing their benefits and limitations. It also reviews and summarizes numerous natural healing modalities that are simple yet very powerful in healing diseases. I included the natural healing modalities that helped me recover from my illness and progress to optimal health. I still use a few of them occasionally as preventative measures to maintain my good health.

Holistic versus conventional medicine

Two opposing approaches to health and disease are conventional and holistic medicine.

The conventional approach, known as allopathic, Western, mainstream or traditional medicine views problems as coming from outside the body. According to this view, the cause of disease comes from outside, invades the body, and the person gets "sick." Allopathic philosophy says that when the body has symptoms, such as pain, fever, or nausea, that means the person has caught some bug or some disease and needs to have these symptoms treated, which may actually mean suppressed or covered up. Rather than addressing the root cause, Western medicine often prescribes medications that temporarily suppress symptoms of disease. Suppressing symptoms is not healing! Once the patient stops taking the chemical medications, the symptoms may reappear. If the disease localizes itself in one part of the body and will not go away, then that part of the body may have to be surgically removed. Thus, the allopathic approach can be summed up as disease, symptoms, drugs, and surgery.[70]

The holistic approach, also known as alternative or Eastern medicine, is very different from the allopathic approach. The holistic philosophy says that the cause and cure of all disease lies within the body. The parts of the body are interrelated in ways that are complex and elegantly orchestrated. In most cases, the body can heal itself when it is provided the opportunity. It does this from the inside out, from the brain and spinal cord outward through the nervous system to every organ and cell. For every time you have been sick, there may have been hundreds of times when your immune system conquered a disease without any overt symptoms being expressed. Holistic medicine heals the whole person: body, mind, and spirit.

A good analogy to illustrate the differences between conventional and holistic medicine is that of a person riding a bicycle on a road strewn with nails. Eventually, the person will get a flat tire, and a patch will need to be applied to the tire for the individual to ride the bicycle again. However, the person will eventually ride over another nail, get another flat tire, and require another patch. This process continuously repeats itself until there is no more room for patches. This is like the conventional medicine approach, with symptoms suppressed and covered through medications that may cause more off-target or even adverse effects than the original symptoms. In the holistic medicine approach, the cause of the problem is determined, and the treatment focuses on eradicating the cause. In our analogy, this approach removes the nails from the road.

Conventional medications can heal, but they can also kill. For example, if you take medication for blood pressure, it may negatively affect your bones. So then you will end up taking another medication to treat your bones, which can cause an additional health issue, perhaps with another organ. In a nutshell, medication may help heal one condition in the body, but may harm another body part and cause another condition through off-target adverse effects. Why not look for the cause and replenish the body with the nutrients that are missing and bring it back to balance?

An antacid or an aspirin may soothe your pain, but it does not cure the cause of your symptoms. Headaches, indigestion, fatigue, allergies, anxiety, eczema, high blood pressure, and other conditions are clues to deeper imbalances in your body. Learning to read those clues is a key step in maintaining optimal health. With the holistic approach, the cause is determined and then treatment is given to restore the body and reach balance. Have you ever wondered about the purpose of using medications to lower cholesterol or control diabetes? Wouldn't it be simpler for individuals to merely alter their diets, to switch to low cholesterol or low sugar diets, rather than experience off-target effects that may lead to additional health issues? Even for people who have high cholesterol caused by a genetic predisposition, cholesterol levels can be controlled to a certain extent by a healthy lifestyle.

I strongly believe that conventional medicine is first and foremost a business, and more money is made by prescribing expensive medications. In addition, Western doctors may get kickbacks from pharmaceutical companies, and they may feel threatened by holistic medicine. However, certain medical issues are best handled through conventional medicine approaches first for stabilization, before turning to a natural approach for long-term reversal. Therefore, a combination of both conventional and holistic medicine approaches, or what is called integrative medicine, is likely best. Integrative or functional medicine practitioners integrate conventional medicine and complementary therapies to promote optimal health and to prevent and treat disease by addressing and mitigating causes. Integrative medicine practitioners are generally MDs, meaning medical doctors, who went to traditional medical school but who also took courses in holistic medicine. Under the conventional medicine umbrella, there is also a DO degree, which is a doctor of osteopathy; DOs tend to practice holistic medicine alongside conventional medicine.

My research indicates that holistic medicine practitioners who use natural remedies have higher rates of success in healing patients than do medical doctors who use Western drugs and surgery. Natural remedies have fewer adverse effects than conventional medications. Many people believe that holistic medicine is useful only as preventative medicine, but this is incorrect; it can actually heal.

Cancer is one of the major causes of death in this country and worldwide. It is such a shame to hear that so many people unnecessarily die of cancer every day. Most tumors are treated using conventional medicine modalities, such as chemotherapy, radiation therapy, and surgery. Unfortunately, in most cases, the cancer comes back. For years, people believed that chemotherapy, radiation, or surgery were the only ways to eliminate cancer. Hippocrates Health Institute teaches that there is an alternative way. People tend to think that only medications approved by the FDA are safe, and if there is no medical research to support a therapy, it must be fake. There is currently no scientific evidence that certain foods kill cancer cells, yet the Hippocrates raw vegan diet presents a way to cure cancer and other terminal diseases. I think people need to be more open-minded in general. As you probably know, all medications have off-target (side) effects, and for many medications, the adverse off-target effects are so bad that they are actually unsafe. Chemotherapy kills good cells along with the cancer cells. Why not give the cancer cells what they need to kill themselves?

I know many people who had terminal illnesses, such as cancer, and were able to heal themselves without any chemotherapy or surgeries. Those people attended Hippocrates Health Institute and took part in their Life Changing Program, a detoxification/cleansing program based on juicing and the raw vegan diet. In a nutshell, their program offers cutting-edge diagnostic and healing therapies. If you are interested in more details, inquire directly at the institute. The people I am referring to who were able to heal themselves through this program, refused all conventional treatment methods, including chemotherapy and surgery. They were able to totally heal themselves from cancer after being on the diet for about a year. A significant decrease in tumor size was noticed by most people after a few months, and the tumors completely disappeared after a year. Their conventional medicine doctors were astounded by their healing and the significant improvement of their health. These people reported not only being healed from cancer but also having significant health improvements. I am convinced that our bodies have the ability to heal themselves when they are given the necessary nutrients.

Conventional doctors know about high blood pressure, cholesterol, and diabetes, and they attribute these diseases to unhealthy diets. But what about people like me who ate healthy and led a healthy lifestyle but got adrenal fatigue and POTS anyway? Conventional doctors did not know why I became ill or how to heal me. I am sure that other people around the country and worldwide also have these disorders and are equally frustrated about not getting an accurate diagnosis or the appropriate treatment.

In addition to detoxing and following the raw vegan diet, I used other treatment modalities as an adjunct, to support the cleansing and healing process, including mostly acupuncture, and naturopathic medicine. Obviously, prevention is much easier than treatment. However, when it comes to treatment, holistic medicine offers many different treatment modalities, including naturopathic, herbal medicine, acupuncture, chiropractic, homeopathic, Ayurveda, applied kinesiology, aromatherapy and massage therapies. Massage therapies include Swedish, deep tissue, sports, Thai, Shiatsu, hot stone, reflexology, and aromatherapy as well as acupressure. I next discuss these holistic medicine treatment options.

Naturopathy

Naturopathic practice includes diagnostic and therapeutic modalities, such as clinical and laboratory diagnostic testing, nutritional medicine, botanical medicine, naturopathic physical medicine, homeopathy, and intravenous and injection therapy. Naturopathic medicine is a distinct primary health care profession, emphasizing prevention, treatment, and optimal health through the use of therapeutic methods that encourage individuals' inherent self-healing processes. The practice of naturopathic medicine includes modern, traditional, and scientific methods.[71]

The following principles are the foundation of naturopathic medical practice. Naturopathic physicians believe in the healing power of nature and act to identify and remove obstacles to healing and recovery and to facilitate the patient's self-healing process. The naturopathic physician seeks to identify and remove the underlying causes of illness rather than to merely eliminate or suppress symptoms. Naturopathic physicians follow guidelines to avoid harming the patient by using methods and medicinal substances that minimize the risk of harmful off-target effects. They avoid when possible the harmful suppression of symptoms and work with an individual's self-healing process. Naturopathic physicians take the whole-person treatment approach by considering individual physical, mental, emotional, genetic, environmental, social, and other factors. Since total health also includes spiritual health, naturopathic physicians encourage individuals to pursue their personal spiritual development. Naturopathic physicians also emphasize the prevention of disease by assessing risk factors, heredity, and susceptibility to disease. They believe that preventing disease is much easier than treating disease.[72]

Herbal medicine

Herbal medicines are naturally occurring, plant-derived substances that are used to treat illnesses within local or regional healing practices. These products are complex mixtures of organic chemicals that may come from any raw or processed part of a plant. Herbal therapy is the use of plants for their scent, flavor, or therapeutic properties for medicinal purposes. Plants have been the basis for medical treatments throughout much of human history, and such therapy is still widely practiced today. Herbal medicines are a type of dietary supplement sold as tablets, capsules, powders, teas, extracts, and fresh or dried plants. The scope of herbal medicine is sometimes extended to include fungal and bee products as well as minerals, shells and certain animal parts. People use herbal medicines to try to maintain or improve their health without the off-target effects that conventional drugs have.[73]

Modern medicine often recognizes herbalism as a form of alternative medicine that is not strictly based on evidence gathered using the scientific method. Modern medicine does, however, make use of many plant-derived compounds as the basis for evidence-tested pharmaceutical drugs. Many people believe that products labeled "natural" are always safe and good for them. This is not necessarily true. Herbal medicines do not have to go through the testing that drugs do. However, conventional medications that go through testing are not good for you either. Some herbs can interact with prescription or over-the-counter medicines, so regardless of what medicine you end up taking, consult a health care practitioner. Western and Chinese herbal medicines have some similarities and some differences. Overall, when quality Chinese herbal medicine is properly prescribed, it is effective and has a lower risk than Western pharmaceutical medicines of adverse effects.

Herbal medicine has its roots in every culture around the world. There are many different systems of traditional medicine. The philosophy and practices of each system are influenced by social conditions, environment, and geographic location, but they all agree on a holistic approach to life. Well-known systems of herbal medicine, such as traditional Chinese medicine and Ayurvedic medicine, have as a central idea that there should be an emphasis on health rather than on disease. By using healing herbs, people can thrive and focus on their overall conditions, rather than on a particular ailment that typically arises from a lack of equilibrium of the mind, body, and environment. Traditional Chinese medicine, the traditional medicine system of China, is the second largest medical system in the world, after Western medicine.[74] Traditional Ayurvedic medicine (Ayurveda), the traditional medical system of India and Nepal, is the third largest herbal medicine system in the world today.[75] Botanical medicine has been practiced for thousands of years, and it continues to be of use in the modern, Western world.

Acupuncture

Acupuncture is a key component of traditional Chinese medicine, and it is based on traditional Chinese concepts such as chi, meridians, and acupuncture points. It is a system of complementary medicine that involves pricking the skin or tissues with needles to alleviate both chronic and acute pain and to treat various physical, mental, and emotional conditions. Acupuncture may help ease pain that is often chronic, such as low-back, neck, and osteoarthritis/knee pain. It also may help reduce the frequency of tension headaches and prevent migraine headaches. Although acupuncture is most commonly used to treat pain, it can be helpful for various health conditions.

Originating in ancient China, acupuncture is now widely practiced in the West. It is generally used in combination with other forms of treatment to relieve pain, promote healing, or cure disease. Acupuncture is generally safe when performed by an appropriately trained practitioner using clean needle techniques and single-use needles. Acupuncture is usually practiced by a doctor of oriental medicine (DOM).

Traditional Chinese medicine explains acupuncture as a technique for balancing the energy or life force (also known as chi) that is believed to flow through pathways (meridians) of the body. By inserting needles into specific points along these meridians, acupuncture practitioners believe that any energy blockage will be removed and the energy flow will rebalance. According to the Mayo Clinic, "many Western practitioners view the acupuncture points as places to stimulate nerves, muscles, and connective tissue. Some believe that this stimulation boosts your body's natural pain killers and increases blood flow."[76]

The body has twelve meridians, all but one named according to its corresponding organ: lung, large intestine, stomach, spleen, heart, small intestine, bladder, kidney, heart governor, triple heater, gallbladder, and liver. The functions of these organs have a broader definition in Eastern than in Western medicine.[77]

Chiropractic therapy

Chiropractic therapy is a form of alternative medicine concerned with the diagnosis and treatment of mechanical disorders of the musculoskeletal system, especially the spine. Proponents believe that such disorders affect general health via the nervous system. Chiropractic therapy emphasizes treatment through manual adjustment or manipulation of the spine. Most chiropractors seek to reduce pain and improve patient health as well as to educate people on how they can account for their own health via exercise, ergonomics, and other therapies that treat back pain. Chiropractors focus on the relationship between the nervous system and spine and believe that biomechanical and structural derangement of the spine can affect the nervous system. For many conditions, chiropractic treatment can restore the structural integrity of the spine, reduce pressure on the sensitive neurological tissue, and consequently improve the health of the individual.

Chiropractic therapy is a health care profession dedicated to the nonsurgical treatment of disorders of the nervous system or musculoskeletal system. Chiropractors generally maintain a unique focus on spinal manipulation and treatment of surrounding structures. They use a variety of nonsurgical treatments to treat patients with certain types of lower back pain, leg pain (sciatica), neck pain, headaches, sports and vehicle injuries, and more. Chiropractors sometimes advise their patients on the use of dietary supplements and diet modifications that they may need.[78]

Homeopathy

Homeopathy is the treatment of disease by very small doses of natural substances that in a healthy person would produce symptoms of the disease. The alternative medical system of homeopathy was developed in Germany at the end of the eighteenth century. Supporters of homeopathy point to two unconventional theories: "like cures like"—the notion that a disease can be cured by a substance that produces similar symptoms in healthy people; and the "law of minimum dose"—the notion that the lower the dose of the medication, the greater its effectiveness. Many homeopathic remedies are so diluted that no molecules of the original substance remain in them.

Homeopathic remedies are derived from substances that come from plants, minerals, or animals, such as red onion, arnica (mountain herb), crushed whole bees, and stinging nettle. Homeopathic remedies are often formulated as sugar pellets to be placed under the tongue although they may also be in other forms, such as liquids, gels, drops, creams, and tablets. Treatments are tailored to each person, and it is not uncommon for different people with the same condition to receive different treatments. It is a helpful therapeutic modality that can help treat many health issues and disorders.[79]

Ayurveda

Ayurvedic medicine (also known as Ayurveda) is one of the world's oldest holistic (whole body) healing systems. Developed thousands of years ago in India, Ayurvedic medicine is based on the belief that health and wellness depend on a delicate balance between the mind, body, and spirit. The primary focus of Ayurvedic medicine is to promote good health, rather than fight disease. Treatments may be recommended for specific health problems. Ayurveda is how your body works to keep you healthy and your unique physical and psychological characteristics combine to form your body's constitution or prakriti. Your prakriti is believed to stay the same throughout your entire life. However, how you digest food can influence it.[80]

According to the Ayurvedic system, a person is made of a combination of the five basic elements found in the universe: space, air, fire, water, and earth. These elements combine in the human body to form three life forces or energies, called doshas. They control how your body works. The three doshas are vata dosha (space and air), pitta dosha (fire and water), and kapha dosha (water and earth). Everyone inherits a unique mix of the three doshas. One dosha is usually more dominant. Each dosha controls a different body function. It is believed that your chances of getting sick are linked to the balance of your doshas.[81]

Ayurveda is a holistic approach to health that allows you to become a balanced, vital, happy person with the least amount of effort. Ayurveda is an ancient solution to our modern-day problems that need quick, effective solutions. I explored following this approach during my recovery to optimal health, but my vata dosha diet recommend mostly cooked vegetables, which contradicted the raw vegan diet I was using at that time, so I decided against following it then.

Applied kinesiology

Kinesiology is the study of body movement. Applied kinesiology, also known as biomechanics or as muscle strength testing, is a method of diagnosis and treatment based on the belief that various muscles are linked to particular organs and glands. Specific muscle weakness can signal internal problems, such as nerve damage, reduced blood supply, chemical imbalances, or other organ or gland problems. Practitioners contend that correcting this muscle weakness can help heal a problem in the associated internal organ. Applied kinesiology can also be used to diagnose and treat nervous system problems, nutritional deficiencies or excesses, imbalances in the body's "energy pathways," known as meridians, and many other health concerns.

The theory of applied kinesiology was developed by George Goodheart, Jr., a Michigan chiropractor who began to write and lecture about his ideas in 1964. Applied kinesiology practitioners are often chiropractors but may also be osteopathic physicians or even conventional physicians. According to the International College of Applied Kinesiology, practitioners must first be trained in their respective fields before they can study applied kinesiology in a postgraduate setting. Applied kinesiology-associated treatments range from deep massage, joint manipulation and realignment, craniosacral therapy, and acupuncture to nutritional therapies and dietary manipulation.

Although the use of applied kinesiology has been suggested for abdominal pain, diabetes, headache, learning disabilities, cancer, and osteoporosis, scientific evidence demonstrating its effectiveness for treating these conditions is limited.

When applied kinesiology is used to determine whether a particular food or other substance weakens (or strengthens) a patient, the food may be placed under the tongue or held in the hand as a muscle is tested. Some practitioners may also assess emotional well-being by testing muscle strength while the patient imagines being in a troubling or tense situation or with a problematic person.[82]

Aromatherapy

Aromatherapy is the use of essential oils from plants for healing. Essential oils are concentrated extracts taken from the roots, leaves, seeds, or blossoms of plants. Each essential oil contains its own mix of active ingredients, and this mix determines what the oil is used for. Some oils are used to promote physical healing, for example, to treat swelling or fungal infections. Others are used for their emotional value; they may enhance relaxation or make a room smell pleasant.

Essential oils have amazing healing properties and can be taken aromatically, topically, or very rarely internally. Most topical and inhaled essential oils are considered safe, especially when they are inhaled. It is recommended to add water or a base or carrier massage oil (such as almond, sesame, or grape-seed oil) to the essential oil before applying to your skin to avoid skin irritation. Avoid using essential oils near your eyes.

Essential oils are very rarely taken by mouth. You should never take essential oils by mouth without specific instruction from a trained and qualified specialist. Some oils are toxic, and taking them by mouth could be fatal. There are companies that prepare formulas of certain ingredients, such as herbs, and mix them with essential oils to maximize absorption.

Researchers are not entirely clear on how aromatherapy works. Some experts believe our sense of smell may play a role. The "smell" receptors in your nose communicate with the parts of your brain that serve as storehouses for emotions and memories. When you breathe in essential oil molecules, some researchers believe that the molecules stimulate those parts of your brain and influence physical, emotional, and mental health. Other researchers think that molecules from essential oils may interact in the blood with hormones or enzymes.[83]

In general, aromatherapy appears to relieve pain and promote a sense of relaxation, improving mood, insomnia, skin conditions, and more. Several essential oils, including lavender, rose, orange, bergamot, lemon, and sandalwood, have been shown to relieve anxiety, stress, and depression. My favorite essential oils are grapefruit and bergamot because of their gentle scents.

As with any other holistic healing modalities, not everyone should use aromatherapy. Pregnant women, people with severe asthma, and people with a history of allergies should use essential oils only under the guidance of a trained professional.

Healing Modalities Conclusion

Some of the aforementioned holistic modalities may be more reliable than others in terms of diagnosis and treatment. These healing modalities are usually used in conjunction with others. For example, acupuncture is often used along with Chinese herbs for healing. There is skepticism regarding holistic and alternative medicine because it is a threat to conventional medicine. Only people who have used holistic medicine can attest to the fact that it helped them heal and they found it beneficial.

There are many good therapists as well as health care professionals or doctors who offer services in the healing modalities discussed here. It is imperative to work with someone who is credible and well qualified and who has good credentials. You should also choose to work with health care professionals who listen patiently and take the time to guide you through the process of healing your body.

In my opinion, it is important to integrate preventive/holistic medicine into every medical school curriculum. I am aware of three universities, the University of Miami, Temple University, and the University of Arizona, that currently offer courses in integrative medicine, although there may be others that offer it now or plan to in the near future. Most people today are knowledgeable about off-target adverse effects and the long-term damage that conventional medications can have on their health and prefer not to take them. Rather than teach medical students how to prescribe medications to suppress symptoms, I think that more holistic methods should be integrated into their programs to help them to think beyond conventional Western medicine. My hope is that conventional and holistic doctors will start working together for the benefit of the patient. I also encourage people to educate themselves, become more knowledgeable, take charge of their health, and realize that they can control their own health by acquiring healthy habits.

Massage Therapies

I discuss in this last section of this chapter several common massage therapies. However, I caution that everyone, especially pregnant women, should check with a doctor before getting any type of massage. I often get massages because I do not consider massage therapy a luxury but a necessary part of a healthy lifestyle. Two of my favorites are reflexology and deep tissue massage because I find them very beneficial for relieving stress and pain.

Swedish

Swedish massage therapy is the most common type of massage. One of its primary goals is to relax the entire body, but this style of massage goes beyond relaxation. Swedish massage is exceptionally beneficial for increasing the level of oxygen in the blood, decreasing muscle toxins, and improving circulation and flexibility in the body. It involves soft, long, kneading strokes, as well as light, rhythmic, tapping strokes in the direction of blood returning to the heart. By relieving muscle tension, Swedish therapy can be both relaxing and energizing, and it may even help after an injury.

Deep tissue

Deep tissue massage is best for giving attention to certain painful, stiff "trouble spots" in your body. The massage therapist uses slow, deliberate strokes that focus pressure on layers of muscles, tendons, or other tissues deep under your skin. Though less rhythmic than other types of massage, deep tissue massage can be quite therapeutic, relieving chronic patterns of tension and helping with muscle injuries, such as whiplash or back sprain.

Sports

Sports massage was developed to help with muscle systems used for a particular sport. Sports massage uses a variety of approaches to help athletes in training before, during, or after sports events. You might use it to promote flexibility and help prevent athletic injuries. Or, it may help muscle strains, aiding healing and recovery after a sports injury.[84]

Thai

Thai massage is a much more rigorous form of massage than its classic Swedish counterpart. Thai massage is also known as Thai yoga massage because therapists will manipulate your body into a series of stretches while working parts of the body with their hands, feet, legs, and knees. During a Thai massage, the therapist uses his or her body to move the client into a variety of positions. This type of massage includes compression of muscles, mobilization of joints, and acupressure. The benefits of Thai massage include relaxation, reduced stress, improved circulation, increased energy and flexibility, and centering of the body and mind.[85] I found Thai massage to be very effective.

Shiatsu

In Shiatsu therapy, pressure with thumbs, hands, elbows, knees, or feet is applied to pressure points on the body. A Shiatsu massage therapist uses varied rhythmic pressure on certain precise points of the body. These points are called acupressure points or meridians, and they are believed to be important for the flow of the body's vital energy, called chi. Supporters say Shiatsu massage can help relieve blockages at these acupressure points. Shiatsu massage has many benefits to the body and mind, including restoring the body's energy, reducing stress, relieving headaches, and helping with respiratory problems, sleep issues, and digestive disorders.[86]

Hot stone

For this kind of massage, the therapist places smooth, heated stones on certain areas of the body, such as acupressure points. The stones may be used as massage tools or be temporarily left in place. Used

along with other massage techniques, hot stones can be quite soothing and relaxing as they transmit heat deep into the body. That helps
warm up tight muscles so the therapist can work more deeply and
quickly. Hot stone massage is very beneficial in releasing tension,
easing sore muscles and pain, improving circulation, promoting
relaxation, and more.[87]

Reflexology

According to the Mayo Clinic, reflexology is the application of
pressure to areas on the feet, hands, and ears. Reflexology is generally relaxing and may be an effective way to alleviate stress. The
theory behind reflexology is that nerves in the feet, hands, or ears
correspond to organs and systems of the body. Proponents believe
that pressure applied to these areas affects the organs and benefits
the person's health. Many massage therapists are also trained in
reflexology.

Several studies indicate that reflexology may reduce pain and
psychological symptoms, such as anxiety and depression, and
enhance relaxation and sleep. There are claims that reflexology can
also treat a wide variety of medical conditions, such as asthma, diabetes, and cancer. Reflexology is generally considered a safe healing
modality, although very vigorous pressure may cause discomfort for
some people.[88]

Aromatherapy

Aromatherapy is a popular way of using essential oils; your skin
absorbs the essential oils and you also breathe them in. The oil is
applied to the body in long sweeping strokes that warm the skin and
muscles. Once the muscles are warmed, the massage therapist will
continue with deep tissue massage. Releasing tension from the muscles increases blood circulation and encourages elimination of toxins from the body, which speeds recovery from an illness or injury.
Massage therapy with essential oils may benefit people with many
different emotional conditions and is great for relaxation.[89]

Craniosacral therapy

This therapy was pioneered and developed by osteopathic physician John Upledger, who performed scientific studies from 1975 to 1983 at Michigan State University. Craniosacral therapy is a gentle, hands-on method of evaluating and enhancing the functioning of a physiological body system called the craniosacral system. This system comprises the membranes and cerebrospinal fluid that surround and protect the brain and spinal cord. Using a soft touch practitioners release restrictions in the craniosacral system to improve the functioning of the central nervous system.

By complementing the body's natural healing processes, craniosacral therapy is increasingly used as a preventive health measure for its ability to support resistance to disease. It is effective for a wide range of medical issues associated with pain and dysfunction, including migraine headache, chronic neck and back pain, central nervous system disorders, orthopedic problems, brain and spinal cord injuries, learning disabilities, stress, and fibromyalgia.[90]

Acupressure

Acupressure is a therapy developed over 5,000 years ago as an important aspect of Chinese medicine. It uses precise finger placement and pressure over specific points along the body. These points follow specific channels, known as meridians, the same channels used in acupuncture. According to Asian medical philosophy, activation of these points with pressure can improve blood flow, release tension, and clear blockages in the meridians. This release allows energy to flow more freely through the meridians and promotes healing.

Acupressure therapy can be used to relieve pain, reduce tension in muscles, improve circulation, and promote relaxation. It is often performed by massage therapists and is used for specific conditions, such as headaches and neck and back pain as well as chronic fatigue, fibromyalgia, and mental and emotional stress.[91]

A massage therapist presses and releases lactic acid from muscles, which is the equivalent of toxins, discharging them into the blood stream. Therefore it is important to drink plenty of fluids after a massage to remove and flush the toxins from the body.

Massage therapy summary

Regardless of what massage therapy type you choose, as I mentioned, there are myriad benefits for each. Massage therapy not only relaxes the body and relieves stress, it can heal many other symptoms and alleviate pain. Massage therapy is so beneficial to our health that it should be considered a necessity, not a luxury.

For more information about any of the topics mentioned in this chapter, please refer to the resources section under "Healing Modalities."

- Massage therapy is a necessity not a luxury.
- Holistic medicine is not only preventative; It can heal as well.
- Use of more than one healing modality at a time is ideal.

"Take care of your body.
It's the only place you have to live in."

— Jim Rohn

CHAPTER 10

Final Words

As I mentioned several times throughout this book, a major key to being healthy is to strike the right balance between physical, emotional, and mental health. A healthy lifestyle ensures that your body has an adequate supply of nutrients that gives you the fuel to live and function. Our bodies need to be nurtured on physical, emotional, and mental levels for us to reach optimal health. When you make the decision to take care of your health, consider starting by consulting professionals, such as nutritionists and personal trainers.

Personal trainers keep their clients motivated through exercise programs that include different types of exercise routines. It is always a good idea to have an exercise plan that you can stick to and enjoy. A good exercise regimen challenges you without exposing you to any health risks. Alternate between various activities that can keep you motivated and prevent the monotony of doing the same things repeatedly. Remember to integrate yoga practice into your exercise plan as well as alternate different yoga styles. Create exercise plans with regular moderate workouts. Exercise at a time of the day that is convenient for you, whether that is in the morning or evening. Set a schedule for your exercise routines and adjust your exercise plan according to your fitness goals. Adjust the suggestions and recommendations mentioned throughout this book to your own body. Use the trial and error method to see what works best for you.

Nutritionists help people design diet plans that can fulfill their health requirements. When you choose a diet type, I suggest listening to your body and selecting the diet or the food you eat based on common sense. What may work for one person may not work for another. Also, what may work for you at the age of twenty may not work for you at the age of fifty because our bodies constantly change. Young people can eat many foods that do not have the same effect as they do in people who are older than forty. So do what works for you, as long as it makes you feel good, energetic, and healthy. However, in addition to increasing your consumption of fruits and vegetables, my recommendation for weight loss or maintenance is to eat five small meals per day. Never combine protein and carbohydrates in the same meal, such as a grilled cheese sandwich or fish and chips, because their digestion requires different types of enzymes, which slows digestion. This is especially important for people who are trying to lose weight. Limit your sugar intake and your caffeine consumption and stay away from refined foods.

I think that the vegan diet, mostly raw, along with a blood type diet and gluten-free is ideal, especially after the age of 40. However, being vegan is not for everyone. Try it and see if it works for you. There is no doubt that the vegan diet has many benefits: it not only keeps you young but also helps you lose weight and improves your health. Regardless of the type of diet you end up choosing, ensure that a health care professional is monitoring those changes in your diet, as well as your exercise routine.

Regarding your diet, keeping a food journal is extremely important because it helps you to determine which foods do not agree with your body. If your body does not react well with certain foods, it will give you symptoms, such as indigestion, heartburn, and nausea. If you get such symptoms, then your body is giving you signs that the food is not for you, so eliminate it from your diet. Listen to your body's signals. If you are hungry then eat. If you are tired then rest. Remember that a food that does not cause any issues today may cause issues a year down the road. Our bodies are always changing.

There are different products on the market, especially nutritional supplements that a person can take to lose weight. People who take such supplements may think that they can keep eating unhealthy foods and lose weight; that does not work in the long run. Others eat unhealthy diets and drink alkaline water hoping to become healthy. Still others may try different methods to control their hunger and to lose weight. These people are just cheating themselves and perhaps buying a bit of time until they end up sick. Instead, use behavior modifications techniques guided by a life coach or a hypnotherapist to ensure a permanent change in the way you think about food.

What is your preference? To look good on the outside? What about the inside? Is your goal to have a long life? Are you concerned only about losing weight and not about your inner health? Doesn't it make sense to be healthy on the inside and as a result lose weight and have a great appearance? I would rather be healthy on the inside and have weight loss as a side effect.

Many people eat an unhealthy diet or overeat and then spend many hours at the gym thinking they can lose weight and become healthy, but it does not work that way. Although exercise helps to burn fat, it is important to complement exercise with a healthy diet to notice a difference.

Why wait until you experience pain or gain weight or get sick and take medications? Why not prevent illness? It's so much easier if you can just control the food that goes into your mouth. This will solve most of your health issues or you may never have them. Isn't prevention much easier than treatment? Unfortunately, we are obsessed with food and use it as a source of comfort, especially when we are under stress or in social settings. Change your mind and change your eating habits. Not only you will lose weight, but you will be healthier. If you love yourself, then it's worthwhile.

Life is all about balance. We must learn how to juggle our responsibilities and demands and still keep our bodies healthy. The key to living in balance is to do everything in moderation. The best healing recipe is a combination of a healthy diet, physical activity, and mind and stress control techniques enriched with nutritional supplements, natural remedies, rest, and most importantly sleep. Our body repairs and heals itself while we sleep. It is a good idea to get at least seven to eight hours of restful sleep at night and take a cat nap or just meditate for a few minutes during the day. Sleep is crucial to all aspects of our lives. When we get a good night's sleep, not only does the body rejuvenates itself, it also restores hormonal balance, lowers stress, improves your mood, and keeps you energized. However, sleep may be a challenge when the body is under stress because stress is known to interfere with sleep. Sleep deprivation can make us more sensitive to stressful events, so keep sleep a priority. It is best to create a bedtime routine, such as listening to relaxing music, avoiding activities such as watching TV, working on the computer, or exercising. Avoid stimulating foods or heavy meals and beverages such as caffeine and alcohol close to bedtime to ensure you get a good night's sleep.

To maintain a healthy lifestyle, be sure to include stress management activities because stress can have an adverse effect on your general health. It is advisable to lower stress levels as much as possible, whether you choose yoga, working out, meditation, meeting with a friend, etc. As long as you take part in an activity that makes you happy, lifts your spirits, and helps to keep stress under control. It is very important to manage your stress on a regular basis. Do not wait until you go on vacation to relax. To avoid burnout, you must integrate stress management techniques into your daily routine. You must examine your reactions to stressful situations or events. Do you tend to put too much on your plate? Do you have overly high expectations of yourself or others? Examine your expectations, and if you let them go, you may not be as disappointed in the outcomes.

As I have mentioned several times, stress plays an important role in healing. It is very simple: regardless of the illness you have, the body does not heal under stress. If all the other areas in your life, such as having a healthy diet, exercising, positive thinking, are satisfied but stress is not under control, you cannot heal. Eating a healthy diet is not enough to keep our body healthy. Once all components (e.g., diet, exercise, nutritional supplementation, and stress) are under control, that is when the body can return to balance or homeostasis. In my case, I ate healthy and exercised but was overstressed and therefore was not fully healed. However, once my stress was finally under control, I reached homeostasis. Stress causes premature aging; it is the number one aging agent. (Second is sugar.)

Yoga benefits our physical bodies as well as our minds and spirits. I hope that someday the benefits of yoga will be recognized in conventional medicine and science.

When it comes to mind control techniques, deep breathing and meditation are an important part of a healthy lifestyle. Regardless of the technique you use, integrate it into your daily life to keep stress under control. There are strong connections between the body, mind, and spirit. Positive affirmations are powerful. Heal your mind and your body will follow! Take deep breaths throughout the day regardless of what tasks you are involved with. You can even meditate while you're washing the dishes or take a few deep breaths while you're watching TV. It is very important to stop in the midst of things and do the breathing exercises, even for two minutes.

All areas of health should be addressed to become healthy and reach optimal health. A healthy diet should be followed first, but all the other components or areas should be addressed as well. All the pieces of the puzzle need to be in place for the picture to be complete and that is when you can reach optimal health. In many instances, people can reverse diseases and heal themselves without medications or surgery. Support and maintain your health by eating nutritious foods, taking nutritional supplements, engaging in physical activity, using stress reduction techniques and any other healing modalities, such as acupuncture or massage therapy, on regular basis. This will ensure that you nourish and repair any problematic areas, restore lost vitality, support your body as whole, and prevent future problems. As a result, your major body systems (respiratory, digestive, immune, nervous, circulatory, etc.) will function optimally and you will reach optimal health.

Eating a healthy diet, exercising, practicing yoga, using stress reduction techniques, and positive thinking helped me to heal myself from POTS and adrenal exhaustion. As I explained in the earlier chapters of this book, I followed the raw vegan diet; I performed various physical activities, including yoga and qigong; I supplemented my diet with nutritional supplements, vitamins, and herbs; I practiced various stress management techniques; I got plenty of rest and sleep. I learned much during that time about my body, about its healing power and the body-mind-spirit connection. I also learned about conventional versus holistic medicine. And most importantly, I learned that we can be our own doctor if we listen to our bodies. I finally realized that if self-care is not my number one priority, I cannot be useful to anyone in my life.

Take an active part in your own healing. Do not count solely on your doctor, who spends only a few minutes during an office visit assessing your condition. Get copies of and review your blood work. Check what is out of the reference or normal range or what is nearly out of range and compare this to your previous test results to find trends. Research and reach your own conclusions. Believe that your body can heal itself if given the proper nutritional support. Keep in mind that prevention is easier than treatment. Do not wait for a health issue to take place in your life. Now is the time to make a change. Following the diet and protocol advice I presented throughout this book will help you in numerous ways. It will help you to look and feel younger, have more energy, lose weight, lower your cholesterol level and blood pressure, reduce your risk of diabetes, and live longer. Take control of your health and well-being. It is in your hands. You deserve to be healthy.

- Disease prevention is easier than treatment.
- Take control of your health and well-being.
- Life is all about balance.

Taly Cotler,
The Stressed Vegan

Dancing always brings a smile to my face.

References

1. DrLam Coaching. Signs and Symptoms: Postural Tachycardia Syndrome. DrLam.com. https://www.drlam.com/blog/signs-symptoms-posturaltachycardia-syndrome-symptoms-adrenal-fatigue/18659/. Published October 2, 2016. Accessed March 2, 2018.

2. Dietary Guidelines 2015-2020 -Eighth Edition. Health.gov. https://health.gov/dietaryguidelines/2015/guidelines/. Accessed February 12, 2018.

3. Health Protocols: Digestive Disorders. Lifeextension.com. https://www.lifeextension.com/Protocols/Gastrointestinal/Digestive-Disorders/Page-04. Published 2018. Accessed March 12, 2018.

4. Dr. Peter J. D'aDamo. Blood Type A. dadamo.com. http://www.dadamo.com/txt/index.pl?1003. Updated May 2, 2018. Accessed May 13, 2018.

5. Heart Health Center. WebMD.com. https://www.webmd.com/heart/. Published November 2, 2016. Accessed March 11, 2018.

6. Campbell TC, Campbell II TM. *The china study*. Dallas, Texas: Benbella Books; 2006. Page 233. Accessed April 22, 2018.

7. Women's Cholesterol Levels Vary with Phase of Menstrual Cycle. Nih.gov. https://www.nih.gov/news-events/news-releases/womens-cholesterol-levels-vary-phase-menstrual-cycle. Published August 10, 2010. Accessed February 20, 2018.

8. What is Celiac Disease? Celiac.org. https://celiac.org/celiac-disease/understanding-celiac-disease-2/what-is-celiac-disease/. Published January 15, 2007. Accessed February 20, 2018.

9. Is the Inflammation Caused by Gluten, Grain, or Both? Glutenfreesociety.org. https://www.glutenfreesociety.org/is-it-gluten-sensitivity-or-grain-induced-inflammation-research-update/. Published 2018. Accessed February 20, 2018.

10. Corwin AK. Carbohydrates and Cholesterol Levels. Livestrong.com. https://www.livestrong.com/article/294152-carbohydrates-and-choles-terol-levels/. Published August 14, 2017. Accessed April 12, 2018.

11. Thistlethwaite F. Eat your way to younger skin: Every time you eat sugar, you gain a wrinkle. Express.co.uk. https://www.express.co.uk/life-style/diets/600925/How-to-get-rid-of-wrinkles-eating-diet-sugar-caffeine-bad-for-you. Updated September 1, 2015. Accessed March 2, 2018.

12. Ulbricht C, Isaac R, Milkin T, et al. An Evidence-Based Systematic Review of Stevia by the Natural Standard Research Collaboration. *Cardiovascular & hematological agents in medicinal chemistry.* 2010;8(2), 113-27. https://www.ncbi.nlm.nih.gov/pubmed/20370653. Accessed May 31, 2018.

13. Cancer. Peta.org. http://www.peta.org/issues/animals-used-for-food/can-cer/. Accessed February 11, 2018.

14. Greger M. Estrogen in meat, dairy and eggs. Nutritionfacts.org. https://nutri-tionfacts.org/video/estrogen-in-meat-dairy-and-eggs/. Published December 24th, 2014. Accessed April 4, 2018.

15. Omega-3 Fatty Acids. Nih.gov. https://ods.od.nih.gov/factsheets/Omega-3FattyAcids-Consumer/. Published March 2, 2017. Accessed March 12, 2018.

16. Parasites. Seafoodhealthfacts.org. https://www.seafoodhealthfacts.org/seafood-safety/general-information-patients-and-consumers/seafood-safety-topics/parasites. Published 2018. Accessed April 4, 2018.

17. What you need to know About Mercury in Fish and Shellfish. Fda. gov. https://www.fda.gov/food/foodborneillnesscontaminants/metals/ucm351781.htm. Published March 2004. Accessed January 14, 2018.

18. Lewin J. The Health Benefits of Eggs. Bbcgoodfood.com. https://www.bbcgoodfood.com/howto/guide/ingredient-focus-eggs. Published 2014. Accessed March 14, 2018.

19. Stanger J. Seven Dangers of Eating Eggs. Perfectformuladiet.com. https://perfectformuladiet.com/plant-based-nutrition/seven-dangers-of-eating-eggs/. Published February 3, 2013. Accessed April 12, 2018.

20. Lactose intolerant? Why most of us can't digest milk. Theweek.co.uk. http://www.theweek.co.uk/64017/lactose-intolerant-why-most-of-us-can-t-digest-milk. Published March 14, 2018. Accessed May 2, 2018.

21. The Casein Cancer Link or Why you Should Ditch that Milk for Good. Nutri-ciously.com. https://nutriciously.com/casein-cancer-connection/. Published October 24, 2016. Accessed April 18, 2018.

22. Andreeva N. 10 Common Food Combinations That Wreak Havoc on Your Health. Mindbodygreen.com. https://www.mindbodygreen.com/0-3615/10-Common-Food-Combinations-That-Wreak-Havoc-on-Your-Health.html. Published December 8, 2011. Accessed May 3, 2108.

23. Triglycerides: Frequently Asked Questions. My.americanheart.org. http://my.americanheart.org/idc/groups/ahamah-public/@wcm/@sop/@smd/documents/downloadable/ucm_425988.pdf. Published April 15, 2011. Accessed May 18, 2018.

24. Low Cholesterol Levels Are Worse Than High? Draxe.com. https://draxe.com/low-cholesterol-levels-are-worse-than-high/. Published December 16, 2009. Accessed April 22, 2018.

25. Medical Definition of Trans fat. Medicinenet.com. https://www.medicinenet.com/script/main/art.asp?articlekey=11091. Updated May 13, 2016. Accessed May 1, 2018.

26. Gold M. Organic Production/Organic Food: Information Access Tools. Nal.usda.gov. https://www.nal.usda.gov/afsic/organic-productionorganic-food-information-access-tools. Published June 2007. Accessed April 5, 2018.

27. Loux R. Top 10 Reasons To Go Organic. Prevention.com. https://www.prevention.com/food/healthy-eating-tips/top-reasons-choose-organic-foods. Published November 3, 2011. Accessed April 14, 2018.

28. Why Organic? 4thgenerationmarket.com. http://www.4thgenerationmarket.com/index.php/articles/why-organic. Accessed May 14, 2018.

29. 15 Amazing Benefits Of Cranberry Juice. Organicfacts.net. https://www.organicfacts.net/health-benefits/fruit/health-benefits-of-cranberry-juice.html. Updated May 16, 2018. Accessed May 22, 2018.

30. The Water in You. Water.usgs.gov. https://water.usgs.gov/edu/propertyyou.html. Updated December 2, 2016. Accessed May 18, 2018.

31. How Common are Kidney Stones. Kidney.org. https://www.kidney.org/atoz/content/kidneystones. Updated January 25, 2016. Accessed May 14, 2018.

32. Timmons M. Don't Confuse pH With Alkalinity. Uswatersystems.com. https://www.uswatersystems.com/blog/2012/06/dont-confuse-ph-with-alkalinity/. Published June 8, 2012. Accessed April 18, 2018.

33. Deziel C. What Is the pH of Distilled Water? Sciencing.com. https://sciencing.com/ph-distilled-water-4623914.html. Updated April 16, 2018. Accessed April 28, 2018.

34. Goldman R, Nagelberg R. Alkaline Water: Benefits and Risks. Healthline. com. https://www.healthline.com/health/food-nutrition/alkaline-water-benefits-risks. Updated July 13, 2017. Accessed 18, 2018.

35. Sugary Drinks and Obesity Fact Sheet. Hsph.harvard.edu. https://www. hsph.harvard.edu/nutritionsource/sugary-drinks-fact-sheet/.   Accessed January 14, 2018.

36. Vitamins and Supplements Center. webmd.com. https://www.webmd. com/vitamins-and-supplements/nutrition-vitamins-11/help-vitamin-supplement. Published November 2, 2016. Accessed February 27, 2018.

37. Misner B. Food Alone May Not Provide Sufficient Micronutrients for Preventing Deficiency. Jissn.biomedcentral.com. https://jissn.biomedcentral. com/articles/10.1186/1550-2783-3-1-51. Published June 2006. Accessed February 10, 2018.

38. Uhland V. Are Synthetic Multi-Vitamins Good for You? Organicconsumers.org.   https://www.organicconsumers.org/news/are-synthetic-multi-vitamins-good-you Published March 15, 2008. Accessed February 20, 2018.

39. Schipani D. Vitamin supplements are mostly a waste of money. Nydailynews.com.   http://www.nydailynews.com/life-style/vitamin-supplements-waste-money-article-1.3004694. Published March 22, 2017. Accessed April 18, 2018.

40. 7 Essential Vitamins You Need After Age 40. Prevention.com. https:// www.prevention.com/health/vitamins-you-need-after-age-40/slide/7. Published October 18, 2017. Accessed May 18, 2018.

41. Nutrition's dynamic duos. Health.harvard.edu. https://www.health.harvard.edu/newsletter_article/Nutritions-dynamic-duos.   Published   July 2009. Accessed April 18, 2018.

42. Meininger K. Side Effects of Echinacea & Goldenseal. Livestrong.com. https://www.livestrong.com/article/362668-side-effects-of-echinacea-goldenseal/. Published October 3, 2017. Accessed January 8, 2018.

43. Schafmeister CE. Molecular Lego. Scientificamerican.com. https://www. scientificamerican.com/article/molecular-lego-2007-09/. Published September 1, 2007. Accessed March 18, 2018.

44. The Top 5 Sources of Toxins You Need to Know About (And What You Can Do to Protect Your Health). Bodyecology.com. https://bodyecology. com/articles/top-5-sources-of-toxins.php. Accessed February 18, 2018.

45. Medical Definition of Stress. Medicinenet.com. https://www.medicinenet.com/script/main/art.asp?articlekey=20104. Updated May 13, 2016. Accessed February 20, 2018.

46. Karriem-Norwood V. Stress Symptoms. https://www.webmd.com/balance/stress-management/stress-symptoms-effects_of-stress-on-the-body#2. Updated July 11, 2017. Accessed April 18, 2018.

47. Lam M, Lam J, Lam C. Adrenal Exhaustion and Other Adrenal Fatigue Symptoms. Drlam.com. https://www.drlam.com/articles/adrenalexhaustion.asp. Accessed March 10, 2018.

48. Silver V. Mind Healing~Can You Heal Your Body with Your Mind? Holistic-mindbody-healing.com. http://www.holistic-mindbody-healing.com/mind-healing.html. Accessed February 23, 2018.

49. what does buddhism teach? Thebuddhistcentre.com. https://thebuddhistcentre.com/text/what-does-buddhism-teach. Accessed May 31, 2018.

50. Thorpe M. 12 Science-Based Benefits of Meditation. healthline.com. https://www.healthline.com/nutrition/12-benefits-of-meditation. Published July 5, 2017. Accessed February 18, 2018.

51. Meditation 101: Techniques, Benefits, and a Beginner's How-to. Gaiam.com. https://www.gaiam.com/blogs/discover/meditation-101-techniques-benefits-and-a-beginner-s-how-to Accessed February 24, 2018.

52. Brunette L. Meditation produces positive changes in the brain. https://news.wisc.edu/meditation-produces-positive-changes-in-the-brain/. Published February 6, 2003. Accessed March 18, 2018.

53. Ambrose A. Deep Breathing Meditation Technique. Livestrong.com. https://www.livestrong.com/article/342513-deep-breathing-meditation-technique/. Published August 14, 2017. Accessed March 18, 2018.

54. Gotter A. Breathing Exercises to Increase Lung Capacity. Healthline.com. https://www.healthline.com/health/how-to-increase-lung-capacity. Updated May 22, 2017. Accessed March 18, 2018.

55. Corliss J. Mindfulness meditation may ease anxiety, mental stress. Health.harvard.edu. https://www.health.harvard.edu/blog/mindfulness-meditation-may-ease-anxiety-mental-stress-201401086967. Updated October 3, 2017. Accessed March 4, 2018.

56. Melton JG. Transcendental Meditation. Britannica.com. https://www.britannica.com/topic/Transcendental-Meditation. Updated March 24, 2008. Accessed March 4, 2018.

57. What is TM? Tm.org. https://www.tm.org/transcendental-meditation. Accessed March 15, 2018.

58. Visualization/Guided Imagery. Mirecc.va.gov. https://www.mirecc. va.gov/cihvisn2/Documents/Patient_Education_Handouts/Visualization_ Guided_Imagery_2013.pdf. Published July 2013. Accessed May 14, 2018.

59. Zimberoff D. What Is the Difference Between Hypnosis and Hypnotherapy? How does hypnotherapy work? web.wellness-institute.org. http://web.wellness-institute.org/blog/bid/256330/what-is-the-difference-between-hypnosis-and-hypnotherapy. Published March 22, 2018. Accessed March 15, 2018.

60. Silva J. Master Your Mind With Silva – And Master Your Life. silvamethod.com. https://www.silvamethod.com. Accessed May 4, 2018.

61. Physical Activity and Health. Cdc.gov. https://www.cdc.gov/physicalactivity/basics/pa-health/index.htm. Updated February 13, 2018. Accessed March 4, 2018.

62. Sutherland S. How Yoga Changes the Brain. Scientificamerican.com. https://www.scientificamerican.com/article/how-yoga-changes-the-brain/. Published March 1, 2014. Accessed March 4, 2018.

63. Walsh S. 7 Yoga Poses to Balance Your Chakras. Mindbodygreen.com. https://www.mindbodygreen.com/0-11865/7-yoga-poses-to-balance-your-chakras.html. Published December 5, 2013. Accessed March 5, 2018.

64. Hatha Yoga. Yogajournal.com. https://www.yogajournal.com/yoga-101/ types-of-yoga/hatha. Accessed May 4, 2018.

65. Vinyasa Yoga. Yogajournal.com. https://www.yogajournal.com/yoga-101/ types-of-yoga/vinyasa-yoga. Accessed May 4, 2018.

66. What is Bikram Yoga? bikramyoga.com. https://www.bikramyoga.com/. Updated December 28, 2018. Accessed May 4, 2018.

67. Ekhart E. The benefits of Yin yoga. Ekhartyoga.com. https://www.ekhartyoga.com/articles/the-benefits-of-yin-yoga. Published November 30, 2017. Accessed May 8, 2018.

68. Eisler M. Nadi Shodhana: How to Practice Alternate Nostril Breathing. Chopra.com. https://chopra.com/articles/nadi-shodhana-how-to-practice-alternate-nostril-breathing. Accessed May 8, 2018.

69. The health benefits of tai chi. Health.harvard.edu. https://www.health.harvard.edu/staying-healthy/the-health-benefits-of-tai-chi. Updated December 4, 2015. Accessed May 8, 2018.

70. Bloom S. Holistic Medicine Vs. Western Medicine. Livestrong.com. https://www.livestrong.com/article/104735-holistic-medicine-vs.-western-medicine/. Published August 14, 2017. Accessed May 4, 2018.

71. Definition of Naturopathic Medicine. Naturopathic.org. https://www.naturopathic.org/content.asp?contentid=59. Updated 2011. Accessed March 3, 2018.

72. Naturopathic Medicine. fnpa.org. http://www.fnpa.org/naturopathic-medicine/. Accessed May 4, 2018.

73. Weil A. Herbal Medicine And Medicinal Herbs. Drweil.com. https://www.drweil.com/health-wellness/balanced-living/wellness-therapies/herbal-medicine/. Accessed May 4, 2018.

74. Traditional Chinese Medicine: In Depth. Nccih.nih.gov. https://nccih.nih.gov/health/whatiscam/chinesemed.htm. Updated March 23, 2017. Accessed May 8, 2018.

75. Herbal Medicine Fundamentals. Americanherbalistsguild.com. https://www.americanherbalistsguild.com/herbal-medicine-fundamentals. Accessed May 7, 2018.

76. Acupuncture. Mayoclinic.org. https://www.mayoclinic.org/tests-procedures/acupuncture/about/pac-20392763. Updated February 14, 2018. Accessed March 4, 2018.

77. A Guide to the 12 Major Meridians of the Body. Remedygrove.com. https://remedygrove.com/traditional/The-Guide-To-The-12-Major-Meridians-of-the-Body. Accessed March 4, 2018.

78. What is Chiropractic? Acatoday.org. https://www.acatoday.org/Patients/Why-Choose-Chiropractic/What-is-Chiropractic. Accessed March 6, 2018.

79. Homeopathy. Nccih.nih.gov. https://nccih.nih.gov/health/homeopathy. Accessed May 4, 2018.

80. Ayurvedic Medicine: A Traditional Knowledge of Life from India that Has Endured the Passage of Time. Anciet-origins.net. http://www.ancient-origins.net/history-ancient-traditions/ayurvedic-medicine-traditional-knowledge-life-india-has-endured-passage-020647. Published December 7, 2015. Accessed March 18, 2018.

81. The Three Doshas: The Keys To Your Individual Nature. Eattasteheal.com. http://www.eattasteheal.com/ayurveda101/eth_bodytypes.htm. Accessed May 4, 2018.

82. Weil A. Applied Kinesiology. Drweil.com. https://www.drweil.com/health-wellness/balanced-living/wellness-therapies/applied-kinesiology/. Accessed May 8, 2018.

83. What is Aromatherapy? Aromatherapy.com. http://www.aromatherapy.com/. Accessed May 4, 2018.

84. French R. Comparison of Swedish, Deep Tissue & Hot Stone Massages. Livestrong.com. https://www.livestrong.com/article/165907-comparison-of-swedish-deep-tissue-hot-stone-massages/. Published July 18, 2017. Accessed March 14, 2018.

85. Cespedes A. Benefits of Thai Yoga Massage. Livestrong.com. https://www.livestrong.com/article/135880-benefits-thai-yoga-massage/. Published January 30, 2018. Accessed May 3, 2018.

86. About Shiatsu. Shiatsusociety.org. http://www.shiatsusociety.org/treatments/about-shiatsu. Accessed May 4, 2018.

87. Lee J. Benefits of Hot Stone Massage. Livestrong.com. https://www.livestrong.com/article/116678-benefits-hot-stone-massage/. Published July 18, 2017. Accessed May 14, 2018.

88. Bauer BA. What is reflexology? Can it relieve stress? Mayoclinic.org. https://www.mayoclinic.org/healthy-lifestyle/consumer-health/expert-answers/what-is-reflexology/faq-20058139. Published September 23, 2015. Accessed May 14, 2018.

89. Boots A. Definition of Aromatherapy Massage. Livestrong.com. https://www.livestrong.com/article/127281-definition-aromatherapy-massage/. Published July 18, 2017. Accessed May 4, 2018.

90. Discover CranioSacral Therapy. Upledger.com. https://www.upledger.com/therapies/index.php. Accessed May 14, 2018.

91. What is Acupressure? Acupressure.com. http://www.acupressure.com/. Accessed May 14, 2018.

Resources

General

www.nutrition.gov
https://draxe.com/
https://www.webmd.com/default.htm
https://www.prevention.com/
https://www.shape.com/

Diet Types

Healthy Tips and Diets

www.heart.org

Mediterranean Diet

https://www.mayoclinic.org/healthy-lifestyle/nutrition-and-healthy-eating/in-depth/
mediterranean-diet/art-20047801

Blood type diet

https://www.4yourtype.com/

Raw vegan diet

https://hippocratesinst.org/

Digestive enzymes

http://www.lifeextension.com/Protocols/Gastrointestinal/Digestive-Disorders/
Page-04

Recommended Foods and Beverages

Sugar Alternatives

https://www.medicalnewstoday.com/articles/316918.php
https://www.medicalnewstoday.com/articles/287251.php

Water

https://www.webmd.com/diet/features/6-reasons-to-drink-water

Vitamins and Supplements

https://www.globalhealingcenter.com/natural-health/synthetic-vs-natural-vitamins/
https://www.fda.gov/ForConsumers/ConsumerUpdates/ucm118079.htm
https://www.naturalnews.com/039638_toxins_ingredients_nutritional_supplements.html
https://www.webmd.com/diet/features/truth-behind-top-10-dietary-supplements#1
https://ods.od.nih.gov/HealthInformation/DS_WhatYouNeedToKnow.aspx

Detox/Cleansing

http://classifieds.usatoday.com/blog/business/10-important-benefits-detoxing-body/

Stress

http://themindunleashed.com/2016/10/how-to-reduce-stress.html
https://www.healthline.com/nutrition/ways-to-lower-cortisol#section1

Adrenals

http://www.nadf.us/
https://aiunited.org/

POTS

http://www.potstreatmentcenter.com/
https://www.ninds.nih.gov/Disorders/All-Disorders/Postural-Tachycardia-Syndrome-Information-Page

Healing the Mind

https://chopra.com/meditation
https://www.webmd.com/mental-health/mental-health-hypnotherapy#1

Physical Activity

https://health.gov/dietaryguidelines/dga2005/document/html/chapter4.htm
https://www.webmd.com/osteoporosis/features/weight-training

Yoga

https://www.thehouseofyoga.com/yang-yoga

https://www.gaiam.com/blogs/discover/a-beginners-guide-to-8-major-styles-of-yoga

Qigong

https://www.qigonginstitute.org/

Healing Modalities

http://www.naturopathic.org
https://draxe.com/homeopathy/
https://ahha.org/

https://nccih.nih.gov/health/ayurveda/introduction.htm
https://www.integrativehealthcare.org/mt/archives/2016/06/aromatherapy-for-emotional-balance.html
https://www.webmd.com/balance/guide/what-is-holistic-medicine#2

33066248R00087

Made in the USA
Columbia, SC
08 November 2018